Fruit & Flowers

IN CROSS

· STITCH ·

Fruit & Flowers

IN CROSS
· STITCH ·

MEREHURST

The charts
Some of the designs in this book are very
detailed and due to inevitable space
limitations, the charts may be shown on a
comparatively small scale; in such cases,
readers may find it helpful to have the
particular chart with which they are
currently working enlarged.

Published in 1994 by Merehurst Limited
Ferry House, 51-57 Lacy Road, Putney
London SW15 1PR

Copyright © 1994
Ariadne/Spaarnestad/Utrecht/Holland
Translation copyright © 1994 Merehurst Limited

A catalogue record for this book is available from
the British Library.
ISBN 1 85391 117 8

Translated by Joké Kramer
Edited by Diana Lodge
Designed by Maggie Aldred
Photography by
Ariadne/Spaarnestad/Utrecht/Holland
Typesetting by BMD Graphics Ltd
Colour separation by Fotographics Ltd,
UK-Hong Kong
Printed in Hong Kong by Wing King Tong Ltd

· CONTENTS ·

Introduction

Cross stitch is perhaps the best-known and most loved of all embroidery stitches, with a tradition going back hundreds of years, and a host of national styles and variations found in countries all over the world. The versatility of this very simple stitch, worked over evenweave fabric, makes it a joy for designers, who can use it to create elaborate pictures or attractive repeat patterns. It was the favourite stitch of our great-great-grandmothers, who used it to make the charming samplers that we still treasure, and is found on the local costumes of Ukranians, Palestinians, Scandinavians and a host of other peoples.

If you have never sampled the delights of cross stitch before, we hope that this book, with its charming theme of fruits and flowers, will convert you. The designs range in complexity, and there are several that a child would enjoy. Each cross stitch design is carefully charted and has an accompanying colour key, together with full instructions for making the project. Also included is a Basic Skills section, which covers everything from how to prepare your fabric and and stretch it in an embroidery hoop or frame, to mounting it ready for framing, while a section at the back illustrates all the stitches used. As you will soon discover, cross stitch is very easy to learn. There are only a few simple rules, and once you have mastered these, you can attempt any design. As with any craft, practice makes perfect, and you will find that perfection is quickly achieved.

If you are already an experienced cross stitch enthusiast, you will be sure to find several projects that will test your skills, rewarding you with an heirloom to be handed down to future generations.

Whatever your level of skill, you will enjoy choosing from the projects in this book, including beautiful samplers and other pictures, cushions, pillowcases and a wide range of elegant tablelinen.

Enjoy your cross stitching!

Basic Skills

BEFORE YOU BEGIN

· PREPARING THE FABRIC ·
Even with an average amount of handling, many evenweave fabrics tend to fray at the edges, so it is a good idea to overcast the raw edges, using ordinary sewing thread, before you begin.

· THE INSTRUCTIONS ·
Each project begins with a full list of the materials that you will require. All the designs are worked on evenweave fabrics, which have the same number of evenly-spaced warp and weft threads per 2.5cm (1in). The fabrics are gauged by the number of holes available for stitching per 2.5cm (1in); for example, 22-count Hardanger has 22 holes per 2.5cm (1in). The two fabrics most used in this book are Hardanger, a fabric originating in Norway and woven with a double thread, counted as one, and Aida, in which threads are bunched into blocks, again evenly spaced, with needle holes at the corners. If you choose to use a different evenweave fabric in place of that specified for a project, this does not matter, provided the fabric is a true evenweave and has the same thread count as the original. The measurements given for the embroidery fabric include a minimum of 5cm (2in) all around to allow for stretching it in a frame and preparing the edges to prevent them from fraying.

Colour keys for stranded embroidery cottons – DMC or Anchor – are given with each chart. It is assumed that you will need to buy one skein of each colour mentioned, even though you may use less, but where two or more skeins are needed, this information is included in the main list of requirements.

To work from the charts, it is often helpful to mark the centre of the design, both on the chart itself and on the embroidery fabric. First count across the chart from the first stitch on the left side to the last stitch on the right. Divide the number in two; count in from one side, marking the centre top and bottom with arrows. Count the stitches running vertically to find the side centre points. Mark the centre of your fabric with two lines of basting stitches, one vertical and one horizontal, running from edge to edge.

As you stitch, use the centre lines given on the chart and the basting threads on your fabric as reference points for counting the squares and threads to position your design accurately.

· W O R K I N G   I N   A   H O O P ·
A hoop is the most popular frame for use with small areas of embroidery. It consists of two rings, one fitted inside the other; the outer ring usually has an adjustable screw attachment so that it can be tightened to hold the stretched fabric in place.

Hoops are available in several sizes, ranging from 10cm (4in) in diameter to quilting hoops with a diameter of 38cm (15in). Hoops with table stands or floor stands attached are also available.

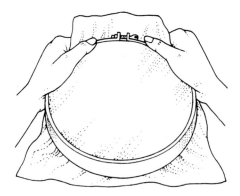

1 To stretch your fabric in a hoop, place the area to be embroidered over the inner ring and press the outer ring over it with the tension screw released. Tissue paper can be placed between the

outer ring and the embroidery, so that the hoop does not mark the fabric. Lay the tissue paper over the fabric when you set it in the hoop, then tear away the central, embroidery area.

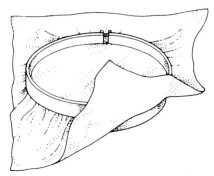

2 Smooth the fabric and, if needed, straighten the grain before tightening the screw. The fabric should be evenly stretched.

· A   R E C T A N G U L A R   F R A M E ·
Rectangular frames are more suitable for larger pieces of embroidery. They consist of two rollers, with tapes attached, and two flat side pieces, which slot into the rollers and are held in place by pegs or screw attachments. Available in different sizes, either alone or with adjustable table or floor stands, frames are measured by the length of the roller tape, and range in size from 30cm (12in) to 68cm (27in).

As alternatives to a slate frame, canvas stretchers and the backs of old picture frames can be used. Provided there is sufficient extra fabric around the finished size of the embroidery, the edges can be turned under and simply attached with drawing pins (thumb tacks) or staples.

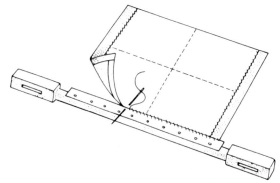

1 To stretch your fabric in a rectangular frame, cut out the fabric, allowing at least an extra 5cm (2in) all around the finished size of the embroidery. Baste a single 12mm (½in) turning on the top and bottom edges and oversew strong tape, 2.5mm (1in) wide, to the other two sides. Mark the centre line both ways with basting stitches. Working from the centre outward and using strong thread, oversew the top and bottom edges to the roller tapes. Fit the side pieces into the slots, and roll any extra fabric on one roller until the fabric is taut.

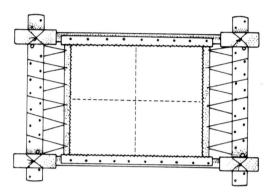

2 Insert the pegs or adjust the screw attachments to secure the frame. Thread a large-eyed needle (chenille needle) with strong thread or fine string and lace both edges, securing the ends around the intersections of the frame. Lace the webbing at 2.5cm (1in) intervals, stretching the fabric evenly.

EXTENDING · EMBROIDERY FABRIC ·

It is easy to extend a piece of embroidery fabric, such as a bookmark, to stretch it in a hoop.

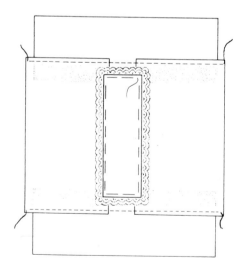

• Fabric oddments of a similar weight can be used. Simply cut four pieces to size (in other words, to the measurement that will fit both the embroidery fabric and your hoop) and baste them to each side of the embroidery fabric before stretching it in the hoop in the usual way.

· MOUNTING EMBROIDERY ·

The cardboard should be cut to the size of the finished embroidery, with an extra 6mm (¼in) added all round to allow for the recess in the frame.

· LIGHTWEIGHT FABRICS ·

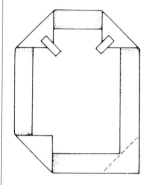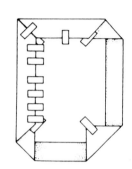

1 Place embroidery face down, with the cardboard centred on top, and basting and pencil lines matching. Begin by folding over the fabric at each corner and securing it with masking tape.

2 Working first on one side and then the other, fold over the fabric on all sides and secure it firmly with pieces of masking tape, placed about 2.5mm (1in) apart. Also neaten the mitred corners with masking tape, pulling the fabric tightly to give a firm, smooth finish.

· HEAVIER FABRICS ·

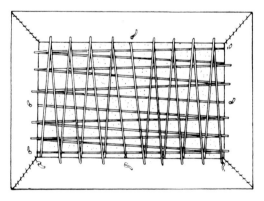

• Lay the embroidery face down, with the cardboard centred on top; fold over the edges of the fabric on opposite sides, making mitred folds at the corners, and lace across, using strong thread. Repeat on the other two sides. Finally, pull up the fabric firmly over the cardboard. Overstitch the mitred corners.

· TO MITRE A CORNER ·
Press a single hem to the wrong side, the same as the measurement given in the instructions. Open the hem out again and fold the corner of the fabric inwards as shown on the diagram. Refold the hem to the wrong side along the pressed line, and slipstitch in place.

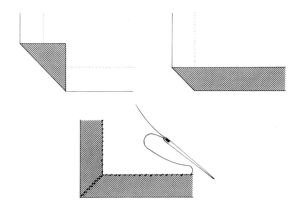

· BACKSTITCH ·
Backstitch is used in the projects to give emphasis to a particular foldline, an outline or a shadow. The stitches are worked over the same number of threads as the cross stitch, forming continuous straight or diagonal lines.

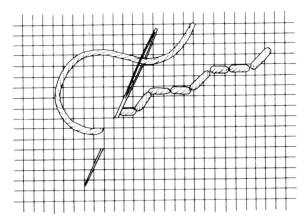

● Make the first stitch from left to right; pass the needle behind the fabric and bring it out one stitch length ahead to the left. Repeat and continue in this way along the line.

· CROSS STITCH ·
For all cross stitch embroidery, the following two methods of working are used. In each case, neat rows of vertical stitches are produced on the back of the fabric.

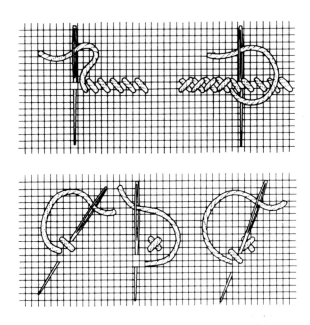

● When stitching large areas, work in horizontal rows. Working from right to left, complete the first row of evenly spaced diagonal stitches over the number of threads specified in the project instructions. Then, working from left to right, repeat the process. Continue in this way, making sure each stitch crosses in the same direction.

● When stitching diagonal lines, work downwards, completing each stitch before moving to the next. When starting a project, always begin to embroider at the centre of the design and work outwards to ensure that the design will be placed centrally on the fabric.

Note All other stitches used in this book are illustrated on page 126.

Yellow & Azure

BREAKFAST · SET ·

Start the day in luxurious elegance with a leisurely breakfast under the shade of a tree. This breakfast set in sunshine yellows and azure blues, with its matching bread cloth and pretty cushion, all decorated with charming cross stitch designs, will surely help to set the scene for a happy day ahead.

· MATERIALS ·

For the **bread cloth**, measuring 45cm (18in) square, you will need:

45cm (18in) square of white, 26-count Hardanger, with or without Aida blocks (see below)
25 × 50cm (10 × 20in) of striped fabric, to tone with the embroidery colours
Stranded embroidery cottons, as listed in the colour key
No 26 tapestry needle
Matching sewing thread

NOTE This design has been worked in Anchor yarns; DMC equivalents are also given, but the end result could be slightly different. The fabric used here featured a woven check pattern in which squares of Aida blocks alternate with Hardanger squares, but a plain Hardanger will be perfectly acceptable if you cannot find this fabric, as the motif is embroidered entirely in a Hardanger area.

For the **cushion cover**, measuring 35cm (14in) square, you will need:

30cm (12in) square of white, 22-count Hardanger
25 × 40cm (10 × 16in) of striped fabric
20cm (8in) square of floral print, to tone with the striped fabric and embroidery cottons
40 × 50cm (16 × 20in) piece of yellow chintz, for the back
1m (1yd) of matching yellow woven tape, 1cm (³⁄₈in) wide
Stranded embroidery cottons, as listed in the colour key
No 26 tapestry needle
Matching sewing thread
A cushion pad to fit

MAKING
· THE BREAD CLOTH ·

From the striped fabric, cut two strips measuring 5 × 45cm (2 × 18in), and two measuring 5 × 47cm (2 × 19in). With raw edges matching and wrong sides together, and taking a 1cm (scant ½in) seam allowance, stitch a short strip to one side of the Hardanger fabric. Bring the strip over the raw edges, turn under the seam allowance and slipstitch to the

Hardanger. Repeat on the opposite side, using the second short strip. Stitch the two longer strips to the remaining sides, turning under the short edges at each corner and finishing neatly.

In one (Hardanger) corner of the fabric, embroider the motif, using two strands of embroidery cotton in the needle and stitching over two (double) threads of the fabric. The leaves of the motif should point towards the striped border, and you should leave 1cm (scant ½in) space between the cross stitching and the striped border. Finish with the back-stitching, again using two strands of thread in the needle.

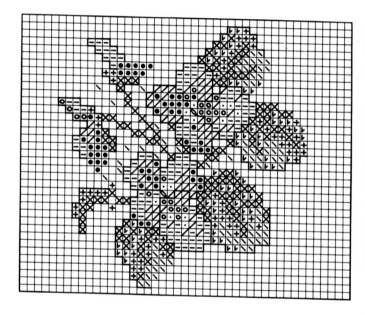

BREADCLOTH ▲		DMC	ANCHOR
⊡	Lilac	209	109
⊟	Light blue purple	794	117
⊡	Very light blue	775	128
◪	Blue purple	793	176
⬤	Dark blue purple	792	177
⊞	Light green	954	203
⊠	Green	912	205
◹	Yellowy green	772	264
⊞	Moss green	3347	266
◪	Yellow	445	288

Backstitching: use dark purple to stitch in and around the flowers; for all other backstitches, use dark green.

MAKING
· THE CUSHION COVER ·

The cushion fabric is embroidered and the side strips are then added. Prepare the fabric (see page 6) and set in a frame. Start at the centre and embroider the cross stitch design, using two strands of embroidery cotton in the needle and working over two (double) threads of the fabric. Finish with the backstitching, using one strand of embroidery cotton in the needle, unless the key states otherwise.

Trim the fabric to measure 22cm (8¾in) square, keeping the motif centred, and then gently steam press the finished embroidery on the wrong side.

· MAKING UP THE COVER ·

From the striped fabric, cut four strips, each measuring 9.5 × 22cm (3¾ × 8¾in). Cut four pieces, each measuring 9.5cm (3¾in) square, from the floral print. With wrong sides together and taking a 1cm (⅜in) seam allowance, join a strip of fabric to each of two opposite sides of the embroidered fabric. Join a square to each end of the two remaining strips, and then join these to the other sides of the cover.

From the yellow fabric, cut two pieces measuring 37 × 20.5cm (14¾ × 8¼in). Taking a 2cm (¾in) seam and with wrong sides together, join the two pieces together at each end of one long side, leaving a 25cm (10in) gap in the middle. Press the seam open; turn under a 6mm (¼in) allowance down the two raw seam edges and stitch them neatly.

To make ties, cut the tape into four equal lengths, and stitch the lengths in pairs to opposite sides of the opening, spacing the ties evenly.

Join the cushion front and back; turn right side out, and insert the cushion pad.

PRIMULAS ▼		DMC	ANCHOR
⊟	Light blue purple	794	117
◪	Blue purple	793	176
⊡	Dark blue purple	792	177
⊠	Green	912	205
⠒	Light yellow green	772	259
⋋	Light moss green	3348	265
⊞	Moss green	3347	266
⠿	Yellow green	472	278
◥	Dark green	909	923
	Black*	310	403

Backstitching: backstitch around flowers with dark blue, flower hearts with black* (used for backstitching only), and work all remaining backstitches with dark green.

Flowered

· BED LINEN ·

This hand-embroidered duvet
cover and matching pillowcase
would be ideal for a guest bedroom.
You can either stitch the motifs
on an evenweave fabric or,
using waste canvas, on easycare
bed linen.

· MATERIALS ·

For the **duvet cover**, measuring 135 × 200cm
(54 × 80in), you will need:

*2.1m (2¼yds) of white evenweave fabric,
140cm (56in) wide, with a pattern of 10-count
Aida blocks and Hardanger blocks
2.1m (2¼yds) of pink-and-white checked
cotton fabric, 140cm (56in) wide
Light pink knitting cotton, no.8
Either poppers or touch-and-close, for fastening
Stranded embroidery cottons, as listed in the
colour key
No 24 tapestry needle
Matching sewing thread*

For the **pillowcase**, measuring 60 × 70cm
(24 × 28in), you will need:

*55 × 95cm (22 × 38in) of evenweave,
as above
55 × 82cm (22 × 32¾in) of checked fabric,
as above
Stranded embroidery cottons, as listed in the
colour key
No 24 tapestry needle
Matching sewing thread*

NOTE The fabric used incorporates 10-count Aida blocks. If you cannot find this fabric, you could use either a different 10-count evenweave fabric, or alternatively you might choose to use the waste canvas technique. For this, decide how many times you wish to repeat the various motifs; you will need to use one piece of 10-count waste canvas for each motif you embroider. For each motif, baste a piece of canvas (approximately 8cm/3¼in square) over the area to be embroidered. Embroider the motif, taking each stitch over one thread of the canvas and through the duvet fabric. When you have completed the motif, unpick the basting stitches, and then carefully remove the canvas threads one by one.

This design has been worked in Anchor yarns; DMC equivalents are also given, but the end result could be slightly different.

· THE DUVET COVER ·

If you are using the original Aida/Hardanger check, withdraw sets of four horizontal and vertical threads, outlining nine-square patches, as indicated by the bold lines on the diagram. Thread the pink knitting cotton through the withdrawn-thread lines, four threads up and four threads down. Embroider a flower motif in each Aida block at the centre of a nine-block patch (if you are not using this fabric, space the motifs evenly, in a similar way). Use four strands of embroidery cotton in the needle and take each stitch over one block. For the backstitching, use three strands of embroidery cotton in the needle.

Place the embroidered top and the pink-and-white checked fabric with right sides together and stitch along the top and sides, taking a 1cm (⅜in) seam at the top, and 1.5cm (⅝in) along each side. At the open end, fold back and hem a double 5cm (2in) turning at each open side. Attach the poppers or touch-and-close fastening and turn the finished cover right side out.

· THE PILLOWCASE ·

Withdraw threads and thread through the knitting yarn, then embroider four motifs, spacing them as for the duvet cover, and leaving 14cm (5⅝in) at one short end undecorated (this will be turned under, to hold the pillow).

On the checked fabric, turn under a double

5cm (2in) hem at one short end. Neaten the raw edge at the undecorated end of the embroidered fabric, and put the two fabrics right sides together, with raw edges matching on three sides. Fold the excess embroidered fabric back over the hemmed edge of the checked fabric. Stitch along the three raw sides, taking a 1cm (⅜in) seam allowance. Neaten, and then turn right side out.

Duvet cover

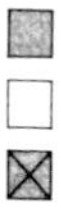

▨	Aida square
☐	Hardanger square
☒	Embroidered square

FLOWERED BED LINEN ▶		DMC	ANCHOR
☒	Dark red	321	13
⊠	Salmon pink	351	10
⊡	Light salmon pink	353	8
◪	Dark pink	601	78
⊞	Pink	603	76
⊟	Light pink	605	74
⊙	Red	606	335
▽	Orange	608	332
◣	Green	701	229
�	Light green	704	238
⦿	Dark orange	900	326

Backstitching: use the darkest colour in each flower for the backstitching, working stitches in and around the flowers

Fruit & Blossom

· CURTAIN ·

Apple blossom and apples, unseasonably but charmingly shown together, make a delightful motif that can be repeated as often as necessary to border a curtain. The curtain shown here has been made from Hardanger fabric and decorated with hemstitching in addition to the embroidered motif, but it would be more economical to embroider the motif on a border strip of Hardanger and stitch this to normal curtain fabric.

· M A T E R I A L S ·

The motif measures approximately 21 × 40cm (8½ × 16in), and the curtain has a drop of 65cm (26in); to make a curtain to your own measurements you will need:

White, 22-count Hardanger, cut to the width and length of the curtain, plus turnings
Stranded embroidery cottons, as listed in the colour key
No 26 tapestry needle
Sewing cotton to match the fabric
Wooden curtain rings

NOTE This design has been worked in DMC yarns; Anchor equivalents are also given, but the end result could be slightly different.

E M B R O I D E R I N G
· T H E   M O T I F ·

Start by working out carefully how many times the motif can be repeated. Space the repeats evenly across the fabric: mark the lower edge of the cross stitch design, 21.5cm (8½in) up from the bottom raw edge of the fabric, with a line of basting stitches, and mark the centre line of each repeat in the same way, allowing at least 5.5cm (2¼in) before the first stitch at each side edge.

Embroider each repeat, starting from the centre and working out. For the cross stitches, work over two double threads of the fabric and use two strands of cotton in the needle throughout. Use one strand of bright pink for the backstitching.

· HEMSTITCHING ·

Make a 12mm (½mm) double hem at each edge and stitch in sewing cotton to match the fabric.

Baste a double 5cm (2in) turning at the top and a double 6.5cm (2½in) turning at the bottom edge. Remove a single thread just below the turning at the top, and four threads just above the turning at the bottom. Finish the hem at the top with a basic hemstitch (see page 126), taking the stitches over two double threads of the fabric, and at the bottom work a ladder variation of hemstitch, taking the stitches over three double threads of the fabric. Use two strands of dark salmon pink for the hemstitching, securing the hems as you work.

With matching thread, neatly finish the sides of the hems, then sew on the curtain rings.

FRUIT AND BLOSSOM CURTAIN ▲		DMC	ANCHOR
⊡	White	White	1
◣	Dark salmon pink	351	329
⟑	Salmon pink	352	328
▼	Dark brown	400	370
⌐	Light brown	422	368
⊙	Moss green	470	267
⊠	Light moss green	471	266
⧄	Dark yellow	725	306
⦂	Ecru	739	275
⊤	Ochre	783	363
⊟	Very light pink	819	271
◺	Light pink	963	24
◢	Green	987	817
⬎	Light green	989	261
⊠	Brown	3045	374
⊠	Dark green	3362	263
⊡	Medium pink	3706	33
⊑	Deep pink	3708	26

Flower Basket

· CUSHION ·

A lavish basket of summer flowers and berries makes a traditional design with timeless charm and beauty, further enhanced in this case by an elaborate cross stitch border.

The cross stitch has been embroidered here on a pale beige fabric, but you could, of course, choose a different colour to tone in with your decor.

· MATERIALS ·

For the cushion cover, measuring 43cm (17¼in) square, you will need:

50cm (20in) square of pale beige, 26-count evenweave fabric
46cm (18¼in) square of plain or patterned fabric, for the cushion back
Stranded embroidery cottons, as listed in the colour key
No 24 tapestry needle
Matching sewing thread
A cushion pad to fit

NOTE This design has been worked in DMC yarns; Anchor equivalents are also given, but the end result could be slightly different.

· THE EMBROIDERY ·

Using four strands of embroidery cotton in the needle and working over three strands of the fabric, begin by cross stitching the borders (see border diagram). Measure up and in from the raw edges by 3.5cm (2½in) at the bottom right-hand corner and embroider border design number I. Repeat this five times, working up to the top right corner. Start at the bottom right again, next to border number I, and embroider number II, working out to the left-hand bottom corner and making three repeats.

Next, work border number III. Start at the top right, above border number I, and work from top right to top left, parallel to border number II, but stopping 30 threads before the end of border number II.

Embroider the remaining side with border number IV, repeating the marked area up to the top edge of border number III.

Finish with the backstitching, using two strands of embroidery cotton in the needle.

Mark the centre of the framed area with horizontal and vertical lines of basting stitches and embroider the flower basket, starting from the centre and working outwards. Use four strands of embroidery cotton in the needle and work over four threads of the fabric.

Finish with the backstitches, made with two strands of embroidery cotton in the needle.

· FINISHING THE COVER ·

Keeping the design centred, trim the embroidery to measure 46cm (18¼in) square, and press gently on the wrong side, using a steam iron. With right sides together and taking a 1.5cm (½in) seam allowance, stitch the cover front and back together, leaving a 30cm (12in) gap at one side. Turn right side out; insert the cushion pad, and slipstitch the gap.

FLOWER BASKET ▶	DMC	ANCHOR
⊡ White	White	1
◎ Yellow	973	279
⊂ Dark yellow	972	298
T Very pale salmon pink	353	86
(Pale salmon pink	352	9
◇ Salmon pink	351	10
▽ Dark salmon pink	350	13
⊠ Red	321	9046
◪ Dark red	304	47
◺ Pink	603	33
◹ Dark pink	601	39
✳ Dark purple red	3685	65
) Very light blue	775	120
◿ Blue green	598	185
⊡ Turquoise	996	186
▲ Dark turquoise	995	188
⣿ Very pale moss green	369	214
T Pale moss green	368	215
◩ Moss green	320	216
◤ Dark moss green	367	217
◿ Light green	704	255
⟏ Bright green	702	239
◣ Dark grey green	501	683
⊔ Light brown	644	853
◺ Brown	642	854
■ Dark brown	611	855
− Yellowy brown	676	943
⊠ Light ochre	436	363
▽ Ochre	435	365
● Black	310	403

Backstitching: stitch in and around the poppies with dark purple red; along the top edge of the basket and along the lower berries, flowers and leaves with dark grey green; around the berries with dark salmon pink, and around the basket and handle with dark brown.

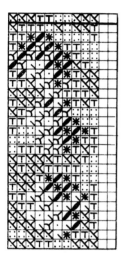

BORDER I ◀	DMC	ANCHOR
⊡ White	White	1
◺ Pink	603	33
◹ Dark pink	601	39
◪ Dark red	304	47
✳ Dark purple red	3685	65
⣿ Very pale moss green	369	214
T Pale moss green	368	215
◩ Moss green	320	216

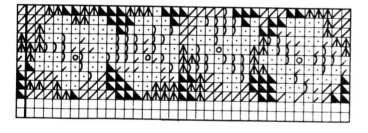

BORDER II ▲	DMC	ANCHOR
⊡ White	White	1
) Very light blue	775	120
◿ Blue green	598	185
◿ Light green	704	255
⟏ Bright green	702	239
◣ Dark grey green	501	683
◎ Yellow	973	279

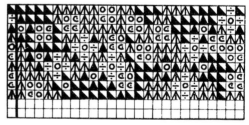

BORDER III ▲	DMC	ANCHOR
◎ Yellow	973	279
⊂ Dark yellow	972	298
⊡ Turquoise	996	186
▲ Dark turquoise	995	188
⟏ Bright green	702	239
◣ Dark grey green	501	683

M

M

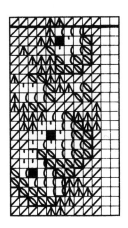

Border diagram

BORDER IV ◄		DMC	ANCHOR
☐	Very pale salmon pink	353	86
◖	Pale salmon pink	352	9
◨	Salmon pink	351	10
◪	Light green	704	255
◩	Bright green	702	239
■	Dark brown	611	855

Backstitching: stitch around the berries with dark salmon pink.

Poppies & Berries

· TABLE SET ·

Bright red poppies with
speedwell and other summer
flowers, embroidered in a circle
on a white checked tablecloth,
have a cheerful elegance that
would make any meal a treat.
Bordered serviettes in the same
fabric complete the set.

· MATERIALS ·

For the **tablecloth**, measuring 135cm (54in) square, you will need:

150cm (60in) square of white, 20-count Hardanger, with a blue check
Stranded embroidery cottons, as listed in the appropriate colour key
No 24 tapestry needle
Matching sewing thread

For each **serviette**, measuring 36cm (14½in) square, you will need:

42cm (16¾in) square of Hardanger, and other materials as above

NOTE This design has been worked in DMC yarns; Anchor equivalents are also given, but the end result could be slightly different.

· THE TABLECLOTH ·

Trim the fabric to measure 145cm (58in) square. On the fabric used here, this left 31 whole checks along each side, plus 7½ for the hem. If your fabric is different, make sure that any pattern is evenly spaced out from the centre. Baste and hem a double 2.5cm (1in) turning on each side, mitring the corners. Embroider the cross stitch border, stitching four (double) threads up from the bottom of the first complete check in the fabric.

Mark the centre of the fabric with horizontal and vertical lines of basting stitches. Embroider the motif from the chart ('M' marks the centre of the fabric), using three strands of embroidery cotton in the needle and stitching over two (double) threads of the fabric. Repeat the motif three more times to complete the circle. Finish with the backstitching, using two strands of embroidery cotton.

· THE SERVIETTES ·

If you are using the same fabric as the picture, there should be 8 whole checks along each side, plus 4½ for the hem. Again, if your fabric is different, make sure any pattern is evenly spaced out from the centre. Baste and hem a double 1.5cm (½in) turning on each side, mitring the corners. Embroider the cross stitch border, stitching four double threads up from the bottom of the first complete check in the fabric.

POPPIES AND BERRIES ►		DMC	ANCHOR
⊡	White	White	1
⊙	Yellow	973	444
⊏	Dark yellow	972	297
◹	Very light salmon pink	353	336
◁	Light salmon pink	352	337
◨	Salmon pink	351	338
⊠	Dark salmon pink	350	339
⊠	Bright red	666	335
⬤	Red	321	46
⊘	Dark red	304	47
	Purplish red*	915	89
⊏	Pink	603	40
⊿	Dark pink	601	42
✳	Dark purplish red	3685	972
⊓	Very light blue	775	975
⊿	Blue green	598	185
⊞	Turquoise	996	433
◪	Dark turquoise	995	410
■	Brown	611	679
⊐	Very light moss green	369	240
⊤	Light moss green	368	241
⊠	Moss green	320	243
◣	Dark moss green	367	263
◺	Light green	3348	253
⊿	Bright green	704	256
◩	Dark bright green	702	258
◤	Dark grey green	501	878
▲	Black	310	403

Backstitching: backstitch around the blue and white flowers with blue green; in and around the poppies with purplish red* (used for backstitching only), and around the salmon pink berries with dark salmon pink.

BORDER ▼		DMC	ANCHOR
⊙	Yellow	973	444
⊡	Turquoise	996	433
◪	Dark turquoise	995	410

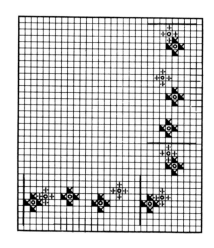

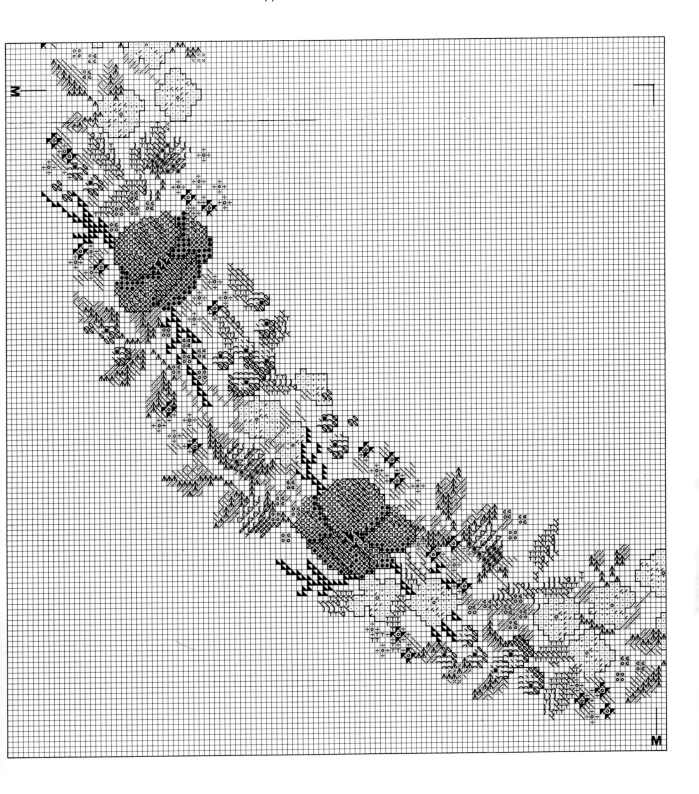

Summer Fruits

· T R A Y C L O T H ·

This charming motif of black
and red currants and damsons
has been stitched on a
traycloth, but it could equally
well be used on a tablerunner
or as a border to be applied to
a guest towel.

· MATERIALS ·

For the traycloth, measuring approximately 30 × 45cm (12 × 18in), you will need:

40 × 50cm (16 × 20in) of white,
22-count evenweave fabric
Stranded embroidery cottons, as listed in the colour key
No 26 tapestry needle
Matching sewing thread

NOTE *This design was originally worked in a thicker yarn; Anchor and DMC equivalents are given here, and a finer fabric has been suggested, so the end result may be slightly different.*

· THE EMBROIDERY ·

Prepare the fabric (see page 6), marking the centre with horizontal and vertical lines of basting stitches, and set it in a hoop or frame.

Starting from the centre and using two strands of embroidery cotton in the needle, embroider the motif, working over two threads of the fabric.

Remove one thread from the fabric 4cm (1½in) in from the raw edge on each side. Make a double 2cm (¾in) turning on each side (the hem level with the withdrawn thread); press and baste. Using matching thread, hem-stitch around the traycloth (see page 126), working over two threads of the fabric.

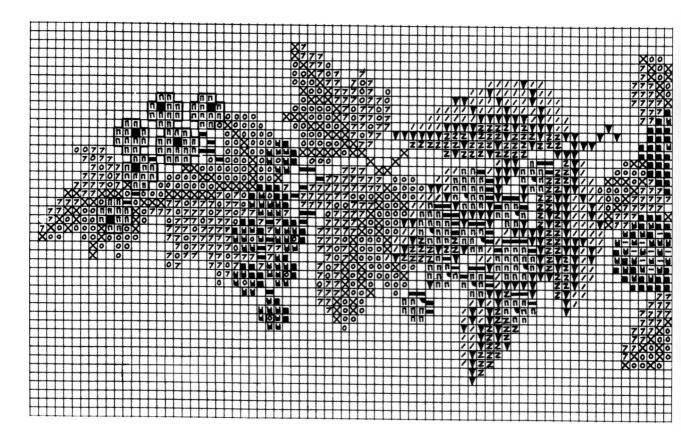

SUMMER FRUITS ▼		DMC	ANCHOR
▼	Dark green	699	923
⊠	Green	700	229
⊡	Olive green	3012	844
⊿	Bright green	702	256
◿	Light bright green	704	254
◺	Light green	3348	253
⊟	Dark red	817	799
⊓	Red	349	9046
■	Dark purple	333	119
⊡	Purple	3746	118
⊟	Blue purple	340	117
⊙	Dark pink	961	38
⊡	Pink	962	31
■	Black	310	403
◣	Ochre	976	363

· T H R E E ·
Flowers

The morning glory, sweet pea
and violet have been celebrated
in three delightful pictures. Just
one would brighten up a dark
corner, and the complete set
would be a delight to own.

· M A T E R I A L S ·

For each picture, measuring 19cm (7¾in) square, you will need:

35cm (14in) square of white, 27-count evenweave linen
Stranded embroidery cottons, as listed in the colour key
No 26 tapestry needle
A frame of your choice

NOTE *This design has been worked in DMC yarns; Anchor equivalents are also given, but the end result could be slightly different.*

· T H E   E M B R O I D E R Y ·

Each picture is made in the same way. Prepare the fabric, as explained on page 6, then work the cross stitches, using two strands of cotton in the needle and taking the stitches over two threads of the fabric. Finish with the back-stitching, again using two strands of thread in the needle.

Gently steam press the finished embroidery on the wrong side; lace it over a cardboard mount, and set it in a frame of your choice.

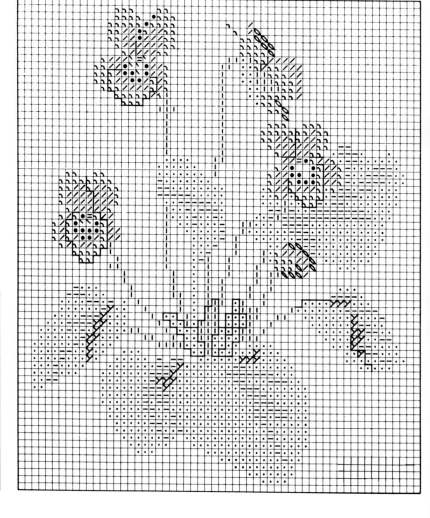

VIOLETS ▶		DMC	ANCHOR
◻	White	White	1
◿	Purple	208	111
◺	Lilac	209	110
◼	Purplish blue	333	119
⊟	Green	702	226
·	Light green	703	238
⊟	Orange yellow	741	303
◎	Dark blue	791	178
⊠	Dark green	910	230
⊥	Very light green	966	206

Backstitching: stitch in and around the flowers with dark blue, and in and along the leaves with dark green.

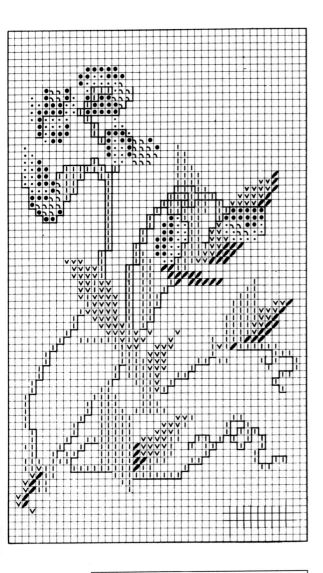

SWEET PEAS ◄		DMC	ANCHOR
☑	Green	702	226
Ⅰ	Light green	703	238
⊙	Rose red	892	28
	Red*	606	46
⧄	Dark green	910	230
◹	Pink	956	54
⊡	Light pink	3708	31

Backstitching: stitch in and around the flowers with red (used for backstitching only), and along the stems and leaves with dark green.*

MORNING GLORY ►		DMC	ANCHOR
⊙	Red	304	799
◹	Rose red	309	42
⊟	Dark pink	335	39
⧄	Light grey	415	398
☑	Green	702	226
⊟	Light green	703	238
⟩	Soft green	722	259
·	Soft blue	775	128
⊠	Dark blue	797	133
	Very dark blue*	820	134
Ⅰ	Blue	799	130
⊚	Light blue	800	159
◹	Pink	899	75
⧄	Dark green	910	230
◺	Light green	966	206
◿	Light pink	3326	75

Backstitching: stitch in and around the morning glories with very dark blue (used for backstitching only), around the pink flowers with red, and along the flower stems with dark green.*

Tomatoes
· A N D ·
Lemons

Tomatoes and lemons make a delicious combination on this summery set of table napkins and cloth, which would be perfect for an elegant kitchen or for lunch outdoors.

· MATERIALS ·

For the **tablecloth**, measuring 155cm (62in) square, you will need:

1.65m (2yds) of white, 22-count Hardanger, 170cm (68in) wide
Stranded embroidery cottons, as listed in the colour key
No 26 tapestry needle
White sewing cotton to match the fabric

For each **table napkin**, measuring 36cm (14½in) square, with a motif approximately 10cm (4in) square, you will need:

40cm (16in) square of Hardanger as above
Other materials, as for tablecloth

· TABLECLOTH ·

Trim the Hardanger to measure 165cm (66in) square, and mark the centre with vertical and horizontal lines of basting stitches. Matching the 'M's on the chart with the basted lines, embroider the motif four times, to make a circle. Embroider the cross stitches over two double threads of the fabric. Use three strands in the needle for the tomatoes, whole lemons, the peel of the half lemons, and the light yellow stitches in the cut side of the half lemons. Use two strands for the slices of lemon and the remainder of the cut sides of the half lemons, and for all remaining cross stitches. Finish with the backstitching, again using two strands.

Make a 2.5cm (1in) double turning on each side, mitring the corners. Press and baste, then remove one double thread just above the folded line, starting and ending 4cm (1¾in) from each corner and using the removed thread to darn in and neaten at each end. Using white sewing cotton, secure the hem with a basic hem stitch (see page 126) taking the stitches over two double threads of the fabric.

· T A B L E   N A P K I N S ·

Make a double 12mm (½in) turning around all four sides and hem as for the tablecloth, then embroider the chosen motif, starting in the bottom right-hand corner, just above the hem-stitching. Use two or three strands of embroidery cotton, as directed for the tablecloth.

Tablecloth

TOMATOES AND LEMONS ▶		DMC	ANCHOR
▯	Bright yellow	307	290
▢	Yellow	444	291
◩	Grey green	562	221
◨	Light grey green	563	219
◪	Red	606	335
	Dark red*	817	13
▲	Bright orange	608	332
⊠	Leaf green	702	239
⊠	Light leaf green	704	237
⊡	Yellowy brown	734	280
⋮	Orange	741	304
−	Very light grey	762	234
●	Blue	799	145
⊠	Dark green	909	228
◹	Green	913	204
◺	Very light green	955	202
◿	Light green	966	241
⊡	Light yellow	3078	293
⊞	Soft orange	3340	329
◨	Light moss green	3348	265
	Dark moss green*	367	263

Backstitching: backstitch around the tomatoes with dark red, in and around the lemons with dark moss green* (starred shades are used for backstitching only), and around the tiles with blue; the remaining backstitches are worked with dark green.*

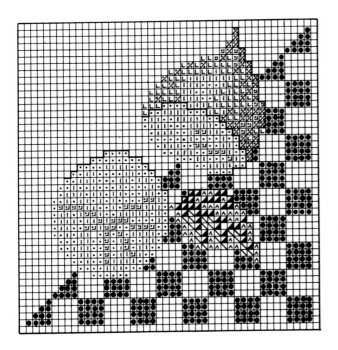

Napkin

Napkin

· A PICTURE OF ·

Gardener's Delight

Here is a sight that would
please any gardening
enthusiast – an abundance of
fruits, vegetables and flowers.

· MATERIALS ·

For the picture, here set in a frame measuring
47 × 55.5cm (18¾ × 22¼in), you will need:

65 × 75cm (26 × 30in) of white, 26-count
evenweave linen
Stranded embroidery cottons, as listed in the
colour key
No 26 tapestry needle
A frame of your choice

NOTE *This design has been worked in DMC*
yarns; Anchor equivalents are also given, but
the end result could be slightly different.

· THE EMBROIDERY ·

Prepare and frame the fabric (see page 6),
marking the centre with horizontal and vertical
lines of basting. Cross stitch from the centre,
using two strands of cotton in the needle,
except for the earth, which is stitched with one
strand only. All stitches are taken over two
threads of the fabric. Finish by backstitching,
using one strand only.

Carefully steam press the embroidery on the
wrong side; lace it over a cardboard mount
(see page 8), and set it in your chosen frame.

GARDENER'S DELIGHT ▶ DMC ANCHOR

⊡	White	White	1
∴	Pale yellow	744	301
⊙	Yellow	742	303
◥	Orange	740	304
☰	Light pink	224	893
C	Pink	3326	51
Ⅱ	Dark pink	335	38
⬈	Purplish pink	3368	66
∨	Light purple	554	96
●	Purple	553	98
⊟	Light salmon pink	352	9
N	Salmon pink	351	10
⊠	Dark salmon	349	13
⠐	Very light blue	828	128
⊡	Light blue	3325	130
⤢	Blue	794	977
◥	Dark blue	931	781
◢	Grey blue	926	850
⟍	Very light green	3348	254
◨	Light green	471	255
+	Moss green	3347	257
▽	Green	989	243
⊠	Dark green	3346	258
⸬	Very light moss green	369	240
�	Light moss green	966	264
◹	Light mint green	368	203
⤢	Grey green	503	215
◖	Dark grey green	502	216
⊡	Light grey	762	234
⟋	Grey	415	399
⟍	Dark grey	318	235
◣	Very dark grey	414	400
⊓	Light brown	437	368
◣	Brown	435	349
◼	Dark brown	400	351
⊏	Light beige	613	831
◪	Beige	612	832
◨	Dark beige	611	904

Backstitching: stitch around the yellow flowers with salmon red; all remaining backstitch lines are embroidered in the same colour or a shade darker than the adjoining area.

Apple Garland

· T A B L E   S E T ·

A garland of russet apples and soft pink blossom circles the centre of this delightful tablecloth, with its set of matching napkins bearing a single apple motif and a matching border of cross stitching. If you do not wish to embroider the tablecloth, apple and blossom motifs could easily be isolated from the design to make a set of tablemats.

· M A T E R I A L S ·

For the **tablecloth**, measuring 135cm (54in) square, you will need:

150cm (60in) square of white, 20-count Hardanger
Stranded embroidery cottons, as listed in the appropriate colour key
No 24 tapestry needle
Matching sewing thread

For each **serviette**, measuring 36cm (14½in) square, you will need:

42cm (16¾in) square of Hardanger, and other materials as above

NOTE This design has been worked in DMC yarns; Anchor equivalents are also given, but the end result could be slightly different.

· THE TABLECLOTH ·

Prepare the fabric and mark the centre with horizontal and vertical lines of basting stitches (see page 6). Embroider the motif from the chart ('M' marks the centre of the fabric, and the motif starts at 'A', 204 double threads away from the centre). Use three strands of embroidery cotton in the needle and stitch over two (double) threads of the fabric. Repeat the motif three more times to complete the circle. Finish off with the backstitching, using two strands in the needle.

Using dark green, and stitching 9cm (3¾in) in from the raw edge, make a line of cross stitches around the border, skipping two (double) threads in between each cross stitch. Fold, press and baste a double turning around the tablecloth mitring the corners; secure the hem at the back of the line of cross stitches.

· THE SERVIETTES ·

For each serviette, using three strands in the needle, embroider the dark green cross stitch border, as for the tablecloth; the finished border should be 33cm (13¼in) square. Embroider a single apple motif in one corner of the fabric, again taking each stitch over two (double) threads.

Turn, press and baste the hem, as for the tablecloth, securing the hem to the back of the cross stitch border.

APPLE GARLAND ▶		DMC	ANCHOR
∴	Very pale yellow	727	305
⊡	Pale yellow	307	290
⊞	Light ochre	725	306
◁	Ochre	783	307
⊘	Orange	970	330
N	Red	349	35
⊠	Dark red	304	19
	Dark pink*	891	39
⊿	Pink	893	38
◩	Pale pink	894	31
⠒	Very pale pink	776	25
·	White	White	1
⊟	Light green	907	254
⫾⫾	Green	470	267
⊠	Dark green	987	211
⊓	Brown	434	370
◼	Dark brown	801	359

Backstitching: for backstitching use dark pink (used for backstitching only).*

APPLE MOTIF ▶		DMC	ANCHOR
∴	Very pale yellow	727	305
⊟	Pale yellow	307	290
⊞	Light ochre	725	306
⌄	Ochre	783	307
◺	Orange	970	330
⊿	Red	349	35
⊠	Dark red	304	19
·	White	White	1
⊟	Green	470	267
⊠	Dark green	987	211
⊂	Brown	434	370
◼	Dark brown	801	359

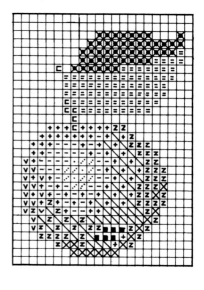

Apple

· CUSHIONS ·

A luscious duo of cushions in rich, autumnal colours, these would add comfort and grace to almost any style of room setting. Alternatively, if the designs were scaled down by making one stitch only for every chart square, you could make an attractive pair of pictures for a kitchen/dining area.

· MATERIALS ·

For the each cushion, measuring approximately 43cm (17in) square, you will need:

46 × 92cm (18 × 36in) of white, 27-count evenweave fabric
Stranded embroidery cottons, as listed in the appropriate colour key
No 26 tapestry needle
32cm (13in) cushion pad

NOTE This design has been worked in DMC yarns; Anchor equivalents are also given, but the end result could be slightly different. If you are making only one cushion, you will not require all the colours listed in the key.

· THE TABLECLOTH ·

For each cover, start by cutting the fabric into two 46cm (18in) squares. Prepare one piece for embroidery (see page 6), and work the cross stitch. Each square on the chart represents *four* cross stitches, instead of the usual one stitch, and each stitch is taken over two threads of fabric. Start from the centre and use two strands of cotton in the needle for all cross stitches. Finish with the backstitching, using one strand of thread in the needle.

· MAKING THE COVERS ·

Both covers are made the same way. Take the plain piece of fabric (back cover) and, with right sides together and taking a 12mm (½in)

seam allowance, join the two together, leaving a gap to insert the cover. Turn the cover right side out and press.

Next, spacing it evenly in from each side, make the border stitches in either green or orange brown. Take the stitches through both layers of the fabric, except at the gap, where the stitches should pass through the top layer only. The finished border should measure 32cm (13in) square. Insert the cushion pad and slipstitch the outer cover and the inner border to finish.

APPLE CUSHIONS		DMC	ANCHOR			DMC	ANCHOR
+	Very light green	472	253	✳ Orange	922	1003
\	Light green	3348	265	‖ Bright orange	742	303
▣	Green	471	254	✕ Yellow	743	295
◪	Soft green	3013	260	◇ Very pale yellow	745	292
■	Dark green	3345	263	≫ Pale yellow	744	293
◎	Light grey green	369	202	△ Soft yellow	677	301
▢	Grey green	368	215	· Ecru	746	2
▼	Dark grey green	320	216	● Dark red	326	19
◆	Dark olive green	732	281	◉ Red	350	13
◈	Olive green	734	279	• Soft red	351	11
	Dark leaf green*	3345	269	− Light red	352	9
◖	Very light brown	676	361	⧸ Very light red	353	6
⬌	Light brown	437	362			
◉	Mid-brown	435	363	*Backstitching: the shades used for back-*		
▣	Dark brown	433	371	*stitching are marked on the charts; dark*		
↑	Orange brown	402	1047	*leaf green* is used for backstitching only.*		

Garden

· S A M P L E R ·

Topiary, urns of flowers, a watering can, a wheel barrow filled with flowers and a host of floral images make this traditional sampler, with its elegant alphabet, a joy to work. Embroidered with some 36 different shades of stranded cotton, this will provide an enjoyable challenge for the cross stitch enthusiast.

· M A T E R I A L S ·

For the sampler, measuring 33 × 49cm (13 × 19½in), in a frame measuring approximately 42 × 57cm (17 × 23in), you will need:

60 × 75cm (24 × 30in) of white, 25-count evenweave fabric
Stranded embroidery cottons, as listed in the colour key
No 26 tapestry needle
A frame of your choice

NOTE *This design has been worked in Anchor yarns; DMC equivalents are also given, but the end result could be slightly different.*

S T I T C H I N G
· T H E S A M P L E R ·

Prepare the fabric and stretch it in a frame, as explained on page 6. Starting from the centre, embroider the cross stitch design, using two strands of the stranded cotton and stitching over two threads of the fabric. For the back-stitching, use one thread of stranded cotton in the needle throughout.

The flowers marked with a large dot are made with French knots (see page 126) as follows: for the pot on the top right, use light pink; for the pot under the arch, use purplish blue; for the pot to the right of the column, use yellow (*this is used for French knots only); use light purplish blue for the pot on the bottom left; use purplish blue for the pot next to it, and alternate these colours for the pot on the bottom right.

Embroider the grasses next to the pots and the stems of the flowers in stem stitch, using two strands of soft green stranded cotton in the needle. For the pots filled with large daisy-type flowers, use detached chain stitches (lazy daisy), with two strands of thread in the needle – purplish blue for the pot on the left of the column and blue for the pot at the bottom left-hand corner. Stitch the centre of these flowers with a French knot, using yellow.

Gently press the finished embroidery on the wrong side, and set it in a frame of your choice.

GARDEN SAMPLER		DMC	ANCHOR
⊡	Light pink	3713	23
⊞	Pink	3326	25
⌊	Lilac	554	90
Ⓝ	Purple	327	98
⟈	Light purplish pink	341	117
◪	Purplish blue	340	118
⊠	Blue	334	140
Ⅱ	Light blue	775	159
⬕	Very light green	369	213
◣	Grey	452	233
⠒	Pale grey	762	234
⊠	Dark grey	413	236
⟋	Green	989	242
⬔	Middle green	987	244
⌂	Light soft green	772	260
⊠	Soft green	3364	261
◪	Dark soft green	3363	262
◤	Very dark soft green	3362	263
⬊	Light yellowish brown	738	361
Ⅱ	Yellowish brown	437	362
⬓	Light beige	3033	391
⫿	Beige	642	392
◣	Light grey	415	399
⫿	Light greeny brown	3047	852
⊟	Greeny brown	372	853
⟋	Dark greeny brown	371	854
◩	Grey green	522	859
◪	Light blue green	503	875
⫿	Blue green	502	876
⠂	Light pinkish brown	950	881
⊟	Pinkish brown	3064	882
Ⅴ	Dark pinkish brown	407	883
⧄	Grey blue	932	920
⋅	Off white	Off white	926
■	Brown	632	936

Backstitching: backstitch in and around the beige-grey pots, the column, the garden bench, the wheel barrow, the watering can and the birds, with dark grey, and in and around the yellow brown and pink brown pots with brown. For all other backstitching, use thread that is just a shade darker than the stitches within the backstitched area.

Fruity

· TABLECLOTH ·

Designed to match the curtain
on page 18, this fresh, pretty
tablecloth would add elegance
to an informal lunch, whether
in the kitchen or in the garden,
and you can repeat the motifs
on a matching set of napkins.

· MATERIALS ·

For the tablecloth shown here, measuring 130
× 185cm (52 × 74in), you will need:

*1.95m (2¼yds) of pink-and-white checked,
27-count evenweave fabric, 140cm
(56in) wide
Stranded embroidery cottons, as listed in the
colour key
No 26 tapestry needle
Matching sewing cotton*

*NOTE This design has been worked in DMC
yarns; Anchor equivalents are also given, but
the end result could be slightly different.
If you cannot find the fabric used here, or a
similar evenweave, you could easily adapt the
design to fit a purchased tablecloth, using the
waste canvas technique described on page 16
(in this case, use 14-count canvas and work
over one thread).*

· MAKING THE CLOTH ·

Start by hemming the tablecloth, making a
double 2.5cm (1in) turning all around, and
mitring the corners. Alternate the apple blos-

som and fruit motifs as shown on the diagram (if your fabric or the dimensions of your cloth are different, adjust the design to suit your needs). Work the cross stitch over two threads of the fabric, using two strands of cotton in the needle. Use one strand only for the back-stitching.

If you choose, you can enhance some of the lines of the cloth (shown as bold lines on the diagram) with lines of cross stitches, made with two strands in the needle and taken over six threads of the fabric.

BLOSSOM ▼	DMC	ANCHOR
● Moss green	470	267
⊠ Light moss green	471	266
◿ Dark yellow	725	306
⊟ Very light pink	819	271
◺ Light pink	963	24
◢ Green	987	817
◹ Light green	989	261
⊠ Brown	3045	374
⊠ Dark green	3362	263
⅃ Bright pink	3706	33
L Light bright pink	3708	26

Backstitching: outline the blossoms in bright pink.

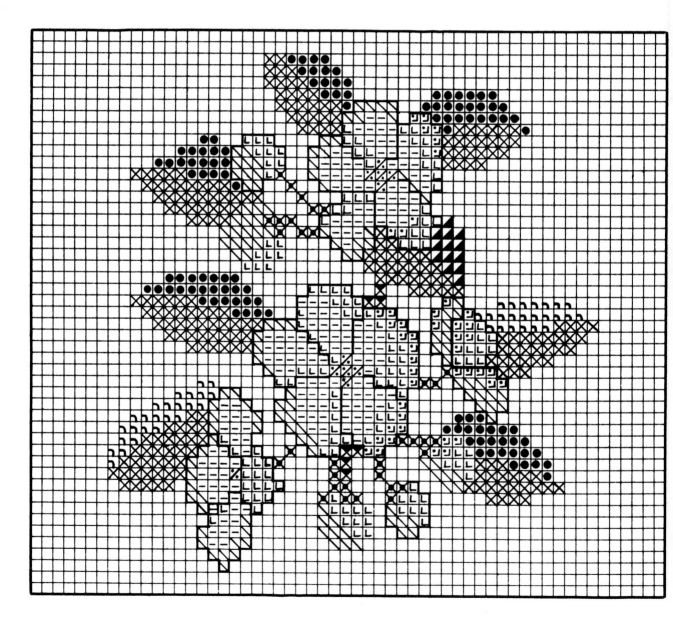

APPLES ▼		DMC	ANCHOR
⊡	White	White	1
◪	Dark salmon pink	351	329
⬓	Salmon pink	352	328
▼	Dark brown	400	352
⬚	Light brown	422	362
●	Moss green	470	267
⊠	Light moss green	471	266
◿	Dark yellow	725	306
⠭	Off-white	739	275
Ⅰ	Ochre	783	363
◣	Green	987	817
◸	Light green	989	261
⊠	Brown	3045	374

A = Apple motif
B = Blossom motif

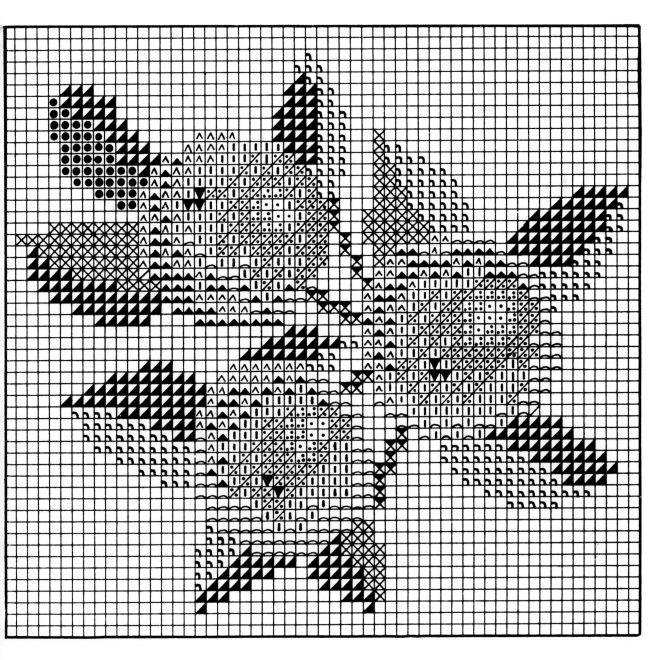

Clematis

CUSHION
· AND ·
TABLECLOTH

This lovely cushion and
matching tablecloth, decorated
with trails of the beautiful
'Nellie Moser' clematis set off
against a yellow background,
would brighten up a dark
corner of any room.

· MATERIALS ·

For the **cushion cover**, measuring 49cm
(19¾in) square, you will need:

*70cm (28in) square of yellow, 20-count
evenweave fabric
52cm (21in) square of yellow medium-weight
cotton, for the back
Stranded embroidery cottons, as listed in the
colour key
No 24 tapestry needle
Matching sewing thread
A cushion pad to fit*

For the **tablecloth**, measuring 124cm (49¾in)
square, you will need:

*140cm (56in) of yellow evenweave, 26-count
fabric
Stranded embroidery cottons, as listed in the
colour key
No 26 tapestry needle
Matching sewing thread*

NOTE This design has been worked in DMC yarns; Anchor equivalents are also given, but the end result could be slightly different. If you are unable to find suitable yellow evenweaves you could dye your own fabrics.

· CUSHION COVER ·

Prepare the fabric, marking the centre with horizontal and vertical lines of basting stitches. Starting from the centre, embroider the cross stitch design, using three strands of embroidery thread in the needle and working over three threads of the fabric. Finish with the backstitching, using two strands of thread in the needle.

Trim the fabric to measure 52cm (21in) square, keeping the design centred. Gently steam press the finished embroidery from the wrong side. Carefully remove two threads along each side, starting 12 threads in from the raw edge in each case. Work an open hemstitch (see page 126) along the withdrawn thread lines, stitching over three threads of the fabric.

Place the front and back cushion cover pieces with right sides together and join, taking a 1.5cm (5/8in) seam and leaving a gap of 30cm (11¾in) at one side. Turn the cover right side out; insert the cushion pad, and slipstitch the gap.

· TABLECLOTH ·

Baste an 80cm (32in) square at the centre of the fabric. Embroider the motif in each of two diagonally opposite corners, making sure that the outermost stitches lie 5cm (2in) in from the basted square. Follow the chart, using two strands of embroidery cotton and stitching over two threads of the fabric. Embroider the left-hand triangular section of the chart only, up to the heavy line.

Finish with the backstitching, using two strands of the embroidery cotton.

Trim the fabric to measure 136cm (44¾in) square. Turn, press and baste a double 3cm (1¼in) turning on each side, mitring the corners. Remove four threads just above the turning, removing them to meet at the corners and then darning in the ends. Secure the hem with hemstitching (see page 126), stitching over four threads of the fabric and using two strands of purple embroidery cotton.

CLEMATIS ▶		DMC	ANCHOR
⊞	Purple	208	112
◪	Lilac	210	108
⊓	Blue	341	117
⊠	Bluish purple	340	118
⦂⦂	Light green	955	240
◁	Green	954	242
⊙	Bright green	913	243
⊠	Dark green	912	244
⦂.	Very light green	3348	253
⸫	Light yellow	3078	300
Z	Ochre	783	307
●	Light brown	782	308
◀	Brown	781	309
⌧	Orange	3340	323
·	Very pale pink	3354	48
⦂.	Pale pink	3373	49
⊟	Pink	604	60
⊞	Bright pink	603	76
⊘	Dark pink	917	78
⫼	Olive green	469	843

Backstitching: backstitch in and around the bottom flowers with bluish purple; the top flowers with bright pink; the flower hearts with orange, and around the leaves use the same colour or a shade darker than the adjoining area.

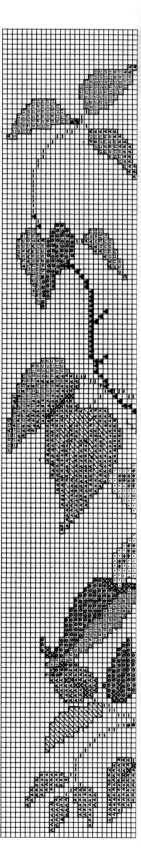

Roses
· S A M P L E R ·

This sampler, with its tubs,
basket, bouquet and garlands is
a joy to stitch – though its
subtle colours demand good
lighting – and will delight you
and future generations.

· M A T E R I A L S ·

For the sampler, measuring 38 × 46cm
(15¼ × 18½in), in a frame measuring
approximately 60 × 65cm (24 × 26in), you
will need:

*60 × 70cm (24 × 28in) of white, 25-count
evenweave fabric
Stranded embroidery cottons, as listed in the
colour key
No 26 tapestry needle
A frame of your choice*

*NOTE This design has been worked in DMC
yarns; Anchor equivalents are also given, but
the end result could be slightly different.*

S T I T C H I N G
· T H E S A M P L E R ·

Prepare the fabric and stretch it in a frame, as
explained on page 6. Starting from the centre,
embroider the cross stitch design, using two
strands of the stranded cotton and stitching
over two threads of the fabric. For the backstitching, use one thread of stranded cotton in
the needle throughout.

Gently press the finished embroidery on
the wrong side, and set it in a frame of your
choice.

ROSES SAMPLER ▶	DMC	ANCHOR
⊟ Lilac	316	969
◺ Yellowy brown	422	943
◪ Green	503	875
⠿ Light green	504	213
⊞ Grey green	523	859
⊺ Light grey green	524	858
◿ Grey brown	642	392
◹ Light yellow	739	880
◺ Salmon pink	758	882
⌐ Pink	760	9
⌐ Light salmon pink	761	968
◺ Yellowy green	772	259
⊡ Light lilac	778	968
∴ Light pink	818	271
· Very light pink	819	892
⊓ Light orange	945	881
◡ Very light orange	948	778
◣ Rose pink	961	38
◥ Dark green	987	244
‖ Light moss green	3031	854
⊠ Dark moss green	3052	860
⊠ Moss green	3053	885
● Deep rose	3328	10
⊿ Light clear pink	3354	74
⊠ Dark grey green	3363	262
⋈ Bright pink	3688	66
⊞ Light pink	818	271
◣ Peachy pink	3712	895
⊓ Deep lilac	3726	970
⊠ Mid-pink	3733	75
◺ Dark salmon pink	3778	883
Light salmon pink	3779	868

Backstitching: stitch in and around the pink and lilac roses with deep rose; in and around the peachy pink roses with salmon pink; around the bows with red, and around the flower pots and basket in dark salmon pink; all other backstitches are in dark green.

Berry

· TABLECLOTH ·

Autumnal berries in rich reds
with dark green leaves decorate
a crisp white tablecloth.
If you choose, the design could
easily be adapted to make an
accompanying tea cosy,
napkins and a cover for a pot of
your home-made jam.

· MATERIALS ·

For the tablecloth, measuring 120 × 160cm (44 × 64in), with an embroidered centre 43 × 63cm (17 × 25in), you will need:

1.7m (2yds) of white, 11-count Aida,
130cm (52in) wide
Stranded embroidery cottons and perle No 5,
as listed in the colour key
No 24 tapestry needle
Matching sewing cotton

NOTE *This design has been worked in DMC yarns; Anchor equivalents are also given, but the end result could be slightly different.*

· THE EMBROIDERY ·

First baste a horizontal and a vertical line to mark the centre of the fabric. Starting at 'M', at one long side of the cloth, 66 Aida blocks from the centre, begin the cross stitching, using three strands of cotton or a single strand of perle in the needle, and taking each stitch over one block. Work the motif (two bunches of berries), and then the corner bunch; turn, and work the motif (two bunches) again, and then another corner, and so on.

When you have finished the central design, make a cross stitch outer border, using the red perle yarn and following the border chart. The finished outer border should measure 116 × 156cm (46 × 62in).

· FINISHING THE CLOTH ·

Trim the cloth to within 6cm (2½in) of the cross stitch border. Turn, baste and stitch a double 2cm (¾in) hem, mitring the corners.

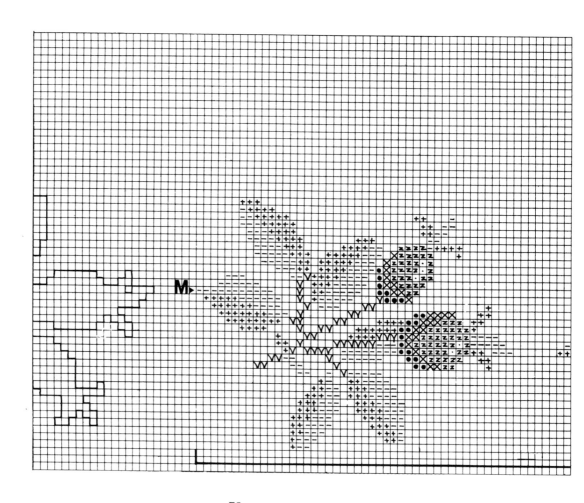

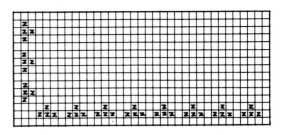

Border design

BERRIES	DMC	ANCHOR
Stranded cotton		
⊞ Green	701	229
⊟ Light green	703	239
Perle		
⊡ White	White	1
⊠ Red	321	13
⊙ Dark red	498	47
⊿ Light red	666	46
▽ Brown	840	379

Motif

Corner motif

Raspberry

· TABLELINEN ·

This mouthwatering set of
raspberry-bordered tablecloth
with matching serviettes and
rings would be delightful to use
on a summer's day, and
decidedly cheering when skies
are dark and wintry.
The tablecloth, like the rings,
is bordered with an edging
stitch which is really a variation
on buttonhole/blanket
stitch, worked in two
interlocking rows.

· MATERIALS ·

For the **tablecloth**, measuring 120 × 170cm
(48 × 64in), you will need:

*1.85m (2¼yds) of pale pink or white,
25-count, evenweave linen
Stranded embroidery cottons, as listed in the
appropriate colour key
No 26 tapestry needle
Matching sewing cotton*

For each **serviette ring**, measuring 4.5cm
(1¾in) deep and 15cm (6in) in diameter, you
will need:

*Two 6.5 × 17cm (2½ × 6¾in) pieces of linen,
as above
Other materials, as above*

For each **serviette**, measuring 40cm (16in) square, you will need:

44cm (17½in) square of linen, as above
Oddment of stranded embroidery cotton, to match
No 26 tapestry needle

NOTE These designs have been worked in Anchor yarns; DMC equivalents are also given, but the end result could be slightly different.

· THE TABLECLOTH ·

Find the middle of one short side of the fabric, and measure in 15.5cm (6¼in). Starting at A, work the motif and then repeat it eight times, leaving out the section left of the line B-C on the last repeat. Turn the corner and repeat the motif again, continuing until you have completed all four sides. Use two strands of embroidery cotton in the needle, and work over two threads of the fabric. Finish with the backstitches, again using two strands.

Embroider the pistils of the flowers with straight stitches and French knots (see page 126), using two strands in the needle. Measure out 9cm (3½in) from the completed border, and work a border of double edging stitch (see page 126), using two strands of pink embroidery cotton in the needle and working over three threads of the fabric.

Trim the fabric, if necessary, to leave it 6cm (2½in) clear of the edging stitch all around. Turn and baste a double 3cm (1¼in) hem and secure it at the back, against the edging stitch border.

· THE SERVIETTE RINGS ·

Each ring is made in the same way. Prepare one of the two pieces of fabric (see page 6) and embroider the raspberry motif in the centre, using two strands of embroidery cotton in the needle and working over two threads of the fabric (the bottom of the raspberry points to one long side).

Take the embroidered and plain pieces of linen, and join each down the short sides, taking a 1cm (⅜in) seam. Turn back and press a 1cm (⅜in) allowance around each long side, and place the plain ring inside the embroidered ring, with wrong sides matching. Finish with a border of four-sided, or double, edging stitch (see below) around the top and bottom of the ring, working through all layers of fabric,

using two strands of pink embroidery cotton in the needle and making the stitches over four threads of the fabric.

· THE SERVIETTES ·

For each serviette, turn, press and baste a double 1cm (⅜in) hem on all sides, mitring the corners. Remove four threads just above the foldline, taking the threads to meet at the corners and darning in the ends. Secure the hem with hem-stitch (see page 126), stitching over five threads and using one strand in the needle.

FOUR-SIDED · EDGING STITCH ·

For this variation on blanket stitch, bring the needle up at the start of the line; take it down a short distance to the right and down, then

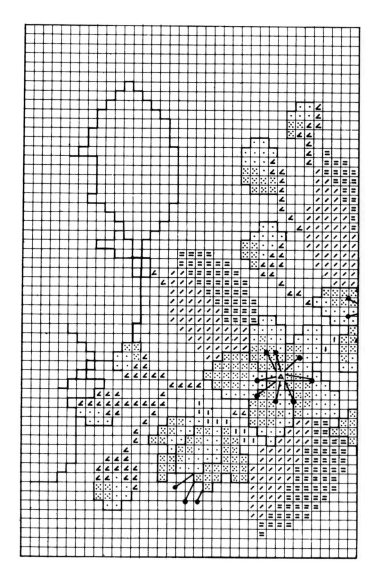

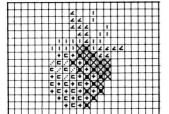

RASPBERRY MOTIF ◄		DMC	ANCHOR
☐	Light green	966	240
◪	Green	913	225
☒	Very dark red	902	72
⊠	Dark red	3350	65
⊏	Dark pink	309	59
⊞	Pink	893	29
⠪	Pale pink	894	27

RASPBERRY BORDER ▼		DMC	ANCHOR
⠪	White	White	0402
⠪	Beige	822	852
☐	Light green	966	240
◪	Green	913	225
◪	Bright green	703	238
⊟	Dark green	701	258
	Moss green*	3052	261
	Yellow*	973	297
△	Orange	971	324
⠪	Light pink	894	27
⊞	Pink	893	29
⊏	Dark pink	309	59
⊠	Dark red	3350	65
☒	Very dark red	902	82

Stitching details: use moss green* for backstitching around flowers; yellow* for the straight stitches, and orange for French knots. Starred shades are used for backstitching or French knots only, not for cross stitches.

bring it up directly above that point, keeping the loop under the needle. Pull the thread through and continue.

To complete the four-sided effect and make the edging, fold the fabric along the line of (blanket) stitches and then work back along the row in the same way from the other side, to make a row of squares, with double threads down the centre and single threads at the top (edge) and bottom.

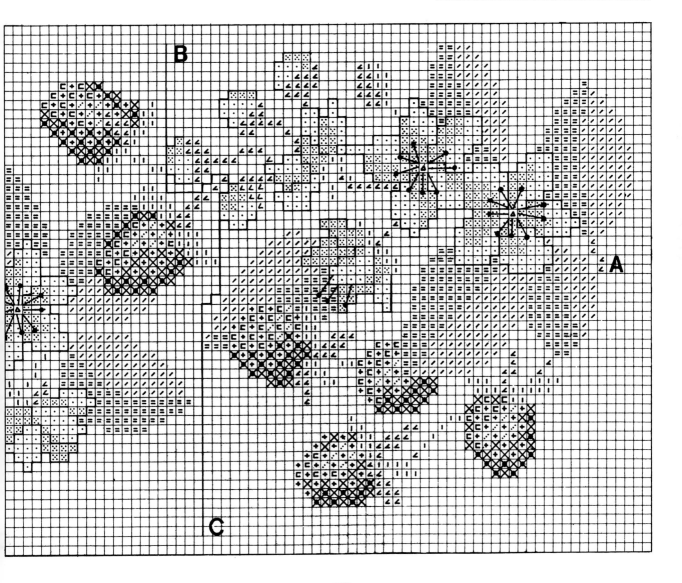

Flowering
· BULBS ·

A beautiful and carefully
observed study of nine bulbs
in flower, this colourful
cross stitch picture is relatively
quick and simple to complete,
for a stunning effect.

· MATERIALS ·

For the picture, here set in a frame measuring
48cm (19¼in) square, you will need:

*70cm (28in) square of cream, 30-count
evenweave linen
Stranded embroidery cottons, as listed in the
colour key
No 26 tapestry needle
A frame of your choice*

*NOTE This design was originally worked in a
yarn that is not readily available; Anchor and
DMC equivalents are given, but the end result
could be slightly different.*

· THE EMBROIDERY ·

Prepare and frame the fabric (see page 6),
marking the centre with horizontal and vertical
lines of basting. Embroider the cross stitch
design: start from the centre and use two
strands of embroidery cotton in the needle. All
stitches are taken over two threads of the
fabric. Finish with the backstitching, using one
strand of embroidery cotton in the needle.

Carefully steam press the finished embroidery on the wrong side; lace it over a cardboard mount (see page 8), and set it in the
frame and mount of your choice.

FLOWERING BULBS ▶		DMC	ANCHOR
−	Light green	955	202
▨	Green	905	239
⊠	Dark green	702	226
⊏	Light bright green	704	254
⋁	Bright green	906	238
⊿	Blue green	912	209
◣	Blue	798	142
⊺	Pink	893	38
⊠	Dark pink	891	39
⊙	Red	349	19
▽	Dark red	816	799
⊠	Orange	947	330
⌞	Light orange	742	303
○	Yellow	743	302
⊿	Light yellow	744	301
⋰	Very light yellow	745	300
⌐	Very light brown	738	366
	Light brown*	437	368
+	Brown	433	371
▲	Dark brown	610	358
■	Very dark brown	3021	904
·	Off-white	712	590
⊤	Mid-blue	813	977

Backstitching: backstitch in and around the lilies with light brown* (used for backstitching only) and orange; all other backstitches are in the same colour as the adjoining area or a shade darker.

Apples &
Pears

· TABLEMAT ·

Apples and pears make a
charming border for a mat that
deserves to enhance only the
very best of home-made apple
pies. The design could easily be
adapted to make matching table
napkins, as in the picture, and
perhaps a set of oblong place
mats as well.

· MATERIALS ·

For the apples and pears mat, measuring 40cm (16in) square, you will need:

50cm (20in) square of beige, 22-count Hardanger
Stranded embroidery cottons, as listed in the colour key
No 26 tapestry needle
Matching sewing cotton

NOTE *This design has been worked in DMC yarns; Anchor equivalents are also given, but the end result could be slightly different.*

· THE EMBROIDERY ·

Using three strands of cotton in the needle and working over two (double) threads of the fabric, work the cross stitching. Begin by making an outer border, 38cm (15¼in) on each side, centering it on the fabric. Embroider a large motif in each corner, and then a small apple motif at each centre point (see the motif layout diagram). Embroider an inner border, enclosing the motifs and completing the frame. Finish with the backstitching, made with two strands of embroidery cotton in the needle.

· FINISHING ·

Trim the fabric to within 3cm (1¼in) of the outer border. Fold over a double 1cm (⅜in) hem, mitring the corners, and sew neatly.

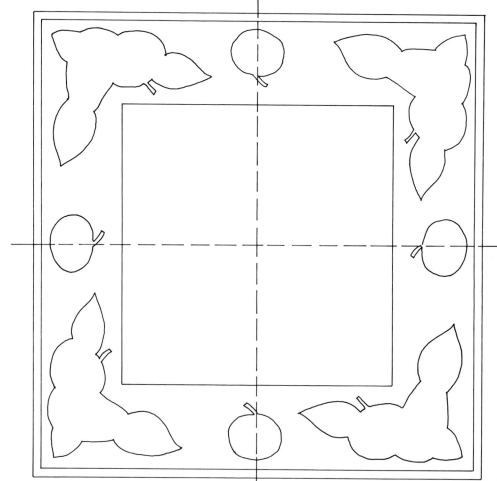

Motif layout diagram

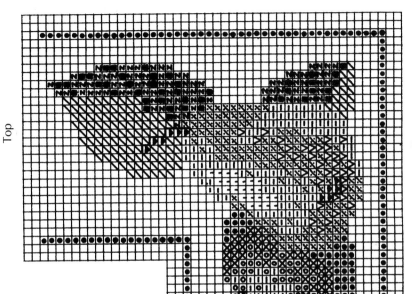

APPLES AND PEARS ▶	DMC	ANCHOR
⊡ Very light yellow	745	301
⊟ Light yellow	743	302
⊠ Yellow	742	303
⊽ Light brown	436	373
▼ Brown	434	374
⊙ Tan	977	308
Dark brown*	838	381
⊠ Dull brick red	921	339
● Brick red	817	13
⊿ Light green	471	266
⊿ Green	367	210
■ Very dark green	935	862

Backstitching: backstitch with dark brown,
used for backstitching only.*

Sweet Pea

· PICTURE ·

A beautiful cross stitch picture
of sweet peas will evoke the
sights and scents of a summer's
garden all the year round.
This lovely design has been
framed as a picture, but it could
be adapted to many uses; for
example, you might like to use
two or three of the stems as
an embroidered edging at one
side of a pillowcase.

· MATERIALS ·

For the picture, measuring 33 × 48cm (13 × 17in), you will need:

50cm (20in) square of white, 27-count evenweave linen
Stranded embroidery cottons, as listed in the colour key
No 26 tapestry needle
A frame of your choice

NOTE *This design has been worked in DMC yarns; Anchor equivalents are also given, but the end result could be slightly different.*

STITCHING · THE PICTURE ·

Prepare the fabric and stretch it in a frame, as explained on page 6. You can start from the centre if you prefer, but for this picture you might find it easier to follow the chart if you start at the bottom right corner, with the letter 'A', placing this 15cm (6in) in from the right-hand edge of the fabric and 12cm (4¾in) up from the bottom edge.

Embroider the cross stitch design, using two threads of the stranded cotton and stitching over two threads of the fabric. For the backstitching, use one thread of stranded cotton in the needle throughout.

Gently press the finished embroidery on the wrong side, and set it in a frame of your choice.

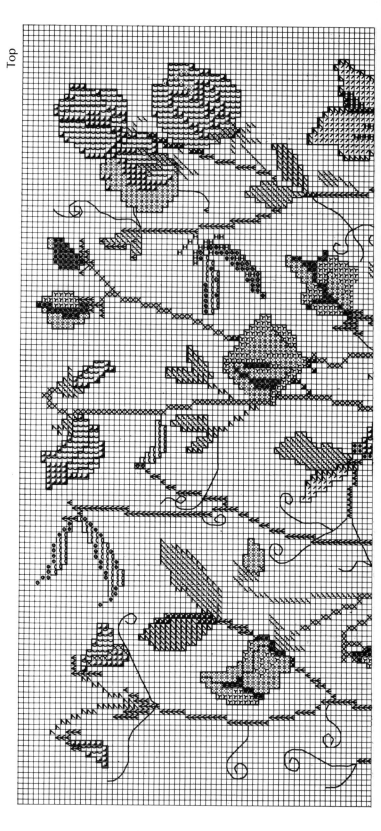

Top

SWEET PEA PICTURE ▶	DMC	ANCHOR
◖ Light pink	963	23
⌐ Pink	3326	25
⊠ Dark pink	899	27
● Rose red	309	39
∷ Light purple	210	108
⊼ Purple	209	109
✳ Dark purple	208	110
◡ Yellow	677	305
⊙ Ochre	680	890
⊻ Light bright green	704	255
⊠ Mid-green	702	257
◣ Light grey green	504	214
⊿ Grey green	503	215
⊤ Dark grey green	501	217
◸ Leaf green	989	226
◤ Dark green	987	245

Backstitching: outline flowers and leaves in a darker shade than the colour enclosed by the backstitching; use leaf green for the tendrils.

Bottom

· BOWL OF ·
Pansies

Here are pansies, almost as
subtly and variously coloured
as the real flowers, to grace
your home in all seasons.

· MATERIALS ·

For the picture, with an embroidered area
approximately 22 × 29cm (8¾ × 11¾in),
here set in a frame measuring 35 × 39cm
(14 × 15¾in):

*50 × 60cm (20 × 24in) of off-white,
25-count evenweave fabric
Stranded embroidery cottons, as listed in the
colour key
No 26 tapestry needle
A frame of your choice*

NOTE *This design has been worked in Anchor
yarns; DMC equivalents are also given, but the
end result could be slightly different.*

· THE EMBROIDERY ·

Prepare the fabric and set it in a frame (see
page 6). Starting from the centre of the chart,
work the cross stitches, taking the stitches over
two threads of the fabric and using two strands
of embroidery cotton in the needle, unless the
key states otherwise. Finish with the backstitching, using one strand in the needle.

Gently press the finished embroidery on the
wrong side; lace it over a cardboard mount
(see page 8) and set it in a frame of your
choice. The one shown here is simple and
modern, but another room setting might
demand a more elaborate frame, perhaps with
a coloured mount.

BOWL OF PANSIES		DMC	ANCHOR
⊡	White	White	2
⊞	Light pink	818	48
◪	Dark red	902	70
◫	Light fuchsia	3608	86
◣	Fuchsia	3607	87
◳	Very pale lilac	3609	95
◳	Pale lilac	554	96
◺	Lilac	553	97
⊠	Dark lilac	552	98
✖	Very dark lilac	550	102
⊡	Light purple	211	108
◱	Purple	209	109
◗	Dark purple	208	110
◢	Dark purple blue	333	119
⊠	Dark blue	792	122
⠐	Light blue	800	144
C	Light grey	762	234
⌐	Very light green	772	259
⊠	Light green	3348	260
◖	Green	3347	261
◣	Dark green	470	267
	Bright green*	986	245
—	Light yellow (one strand)	677	292
⊼	Very light orange yellow	745	300
～	Light orange yellow	744	301
◗	Orange yellow	437	311
◎	Light orange	977	313
⊠	Orange	329	3340
◩	Light pinkish brown	950	376
⊓	Very light yellow	746	386
◿	Light grey brown (one strand)	3033	830
◺	Very light grey blue	3072	847
◤	Light grey blue	928	848
⊡	Very light grey yellow (one strand)	3047	852
⊟	Light grey green	524	858
◺	Grey green	523	859
◉	Dark grey green	3363	860
	Dark grey*	413	236
	Black*	310	403
Z	Light salmon pink	880	951
◖	Salmon pink	950	882
◹	Ochre yellow	676	891
⊡	Ecru (one strand)	Ecru	926
⊠	Blue	334	977

Backstitching: backstitch around the pansies with very dark purple, the leaves with bright green, the vase with dark grey*, and the pansy hearts with black*; starred shades are used for backstitching only.*

Cherries
· A N D ·
Strawberries

Strawberries have been a popular theme with embroiderers since Elizabethan times, and what could be more charming and appropriate for a summer's luncheon than placemats decorated with strawberry plants? To complete the scene, embroider a set of cherry napkins.

· M A T E R I A L S ·

For one **tablemat**, measuring 36 × 48cm (14½ × 19¼in), you will need:

40 × 52cm (16 × 20¾in) of 26-count evenweave fabric, in a colour of your choice Stranded embroidery cottons, as listed in the appropriate colour key No 26 tapestry needle

For one **napkin**, measuring 36cm (14½in) square, you will need:

40cm (16in) square of white 27-count evenweave fabric: Stranded embroidery cottons, as listed in the appropriate colour key No 26 tapestry needle

NOTE These designs have been worked in DMC yarns; Anchor equivalents are also given, but the end result could be slightly different.

· S T R A W B E R R Y T A B L E M A T ·

Prepare the fabric (see page 6). Positioning the stitching 6.5cm (2½in) up from the bottom edge and the same distance in from the left-hand side, embroider the cross stitches, using two strands of embroidery cotton in the needle

and stitching over two threads of the fabric. Finish with the backstitches, using one strand in the needle.

Press and baste a double 1cm (½in) hem around the tablemat, mitring the corners. Remove a fabric thread just above the foldline on each side, then secure the hem with an open hemstitch (see page 126), working over two threads of the fabric and using two strands of embroidery yarn to match the fabric.

· C H E R R Y N A P K I N ·

Prepare the fabric (see page 6), and embroider the cherry motif in one corner. Make sure that the motif lies a minimum of 5cm (2in) in from the raw edge, and work over two threads of the fabric, using two strands of embroidery cotton in the needle.

Turn, press and baste a double 1cm (⅜in) hem all around the fabric, mitring the corners. Remove two threads of the fabric just above the folded edge, so that the withdrawn thread lines meet at the corners of the napkin. Darn in the ends at the corners, and then secure the hem with hemstitching (see page 126), using two strands of light green embroidery cotton and working over three threads of the fabric.

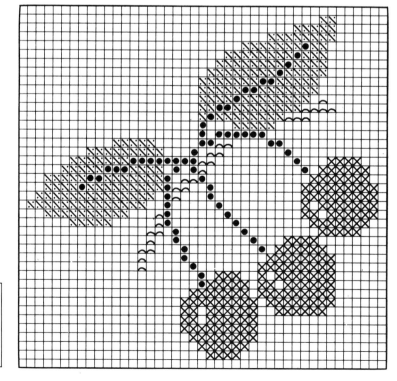

CHERRY NAPKIN ▶		DMC	ANCHOR
⊠	Red	349	9046
◩	Light green	989	266
⦿	Green	986	246
⌓	Brown	3064	373

STRAWBERRY ◀		
TABLEMAT	**DMC**	**ANCHOR**
· White	White	1
○ Yellow	743	306
● Light salmon red	351	328
■ Salmon red	349	333
− Very light green	3348	265
⋁ Light green	3347	267
N Olive green	732	927
L Green	702	227
⊟ Grey green	989	266
✕ Mid-green	988	210
◪ Dark green	986	246
◪ Brown	433	906

*Backstitching: backstitch around the white
flowers with green, in the white flowers
with light salmon red, and make all other
backstitches in a matching colour or a shade
slightly darker than the adjoining area.*

97

· M Y   C O T T A G E ·
Garden

A border of floral motifs
surrounds a country idyll.
With over 50 different shades
of stranded cotton, this is a
challenging piece – a future
family heirloom. You could
either embroider the alphabet
as shown above the cottage,
or alternatively you might prefer
to insert your own name and
the finishing date.
If you do not choose to make
the picture, the flowers around
the border would look most
attractive on a tablecloth.

· M A T E R I A L S ·
For the sampler, measuring 33.5 × 38.5cm
(13½ × 15½in), set in a frame measuring
48 × 52cm (19¼ × 20¾in), you will need:

*65 × 70cm (26 × 28in) of white, 26-count
evenweave fabric*
*Stranded embroidery cottons, as listed in the
colour key*
No 26 tapestry needle

*NOTE This design has been worked in DMC
yarns; Anchor equivalents are also given, but
the end result could be slightly different.*

· T H E   E M B R O I D E R Y ·
Prepare the fabric and stretch it in a frame, as
explained on page 7. Starting from the centre,
embroider the cross stitch design, using two
strands of embroidery cotton and stitching over
two threads of the fabric. For backstitching, use
one thread of cotton in the needle throughout.

Some of the flowers around the cottage are
marked with a dot. Each dot represents a French
knot, worked with two strands of thread in the
needle, as follows: use dark yellow for the hearts
of the white flowers; light yellow for the hearts
of the dark blue purple flowers; light rose pink*
and medium rose pink* (both used for French
knots only) for the panicles, and yellow for
the flowers at the bottom of the central picture.

Detached chain stitch (lazy daisy), embroidered with two strands of thread in the needle,
is used for some of the flowers in the garden;
those to the left of the path are stitched with
white, and those to the right are stitched with
dark purplish blue.

Gently press the finished embroidery on the
wrong side; lace it over firm cardboard, and
set in a frame of your choice.

> *Backstitching: backstitch in and around the house
> with dark grey; around the blue door and window
> frames, in and around the purple blue border
> flowers at the top left and the blue border flowers at
> the bottom right with dark blue*; around the hearts
> of the pink border flowers at the bottom right and the
> door handle with black*; in and around the yellow
> border flowers at the top left with orange red*;
> around the grey white border flower at the top right
> with green, and around the purple border flower at
> the bottom centre with dark purple blue*. For all
> remaining backstitching, use the same colour as the
> adjacent area or a slightly darker shade.*

MY COTTAGE GARDEN		DMC	ANCHOR
⊡	White	White	02
◨	Dark soft green	320	215
◩	Purplish blue	340	118
◨	Light purplish blue	341	117
‖	Light soft green	368	214
◿	Soft green	369	213
▼	Dark grey	413	236
◺	Yellowish brown	437	362
⊠	Mushroom	452	232
◰	Light mushroom	453	231
◹	Blue green	502	876
⊡	Light grey green	503	875
⊓	Very light grey green	504	213
⊞	Greeny blue	518	168
⊠	Moss green	522	859
◸	Light moss green	524	858
◪	Middle grey	647	399
⋰	Cream	712	275
◖	Yellow	726	295
⠶	Beige	739	885
✳	Dark yellow	743	305
⊻	Light yellow	745	300
⋒	Light salmon pink	754	6
	Orange red*	352	9
◿	Old pink	760	894
⊠	Light old pink	761	893
⊡	Silver grey	762	234
⊓	Light green	772	259
	Dark blue*	797	133
◿	Middle blue	798	146
⊙	Soft blue	809	130
◣	Light soft pink	818	271
⬩	Very light soft pink	819	271
◤	Dark pink brown	840	379
◩	Pinkish brown	841	378
⊤	Light pinkish brown	842	376
⊙	Light pink	963	23
◺	Bright green	987	244
⊠	Dark bright green	988	243
⊞	Light brownish green	3012	843
◿	Very light brownish green	3013	842
⊔	Grey	3024	397
◺	Very light brownish grey	3033	390
◡	Very light yellow	3078	292
◼	Dark green	3345	268
⊽	Green	3347	266
⋮⋮	Light green	3364	260
◤	Purplish pink	3688	76
◥	Light purplish pink	3689	74
⋰	Very light purplish pink	3713	73
⊠	Dark rose pink	3731	76
◤	Rose pink	3733	75
	Medium rose pink*	962	75
	Light rose pink *	3716	50
	Dark purplish blue*	3746	119
◺	Pale purplish blue	3747	120
◺	Pinkish brown	3772	914
	Black*	310	403

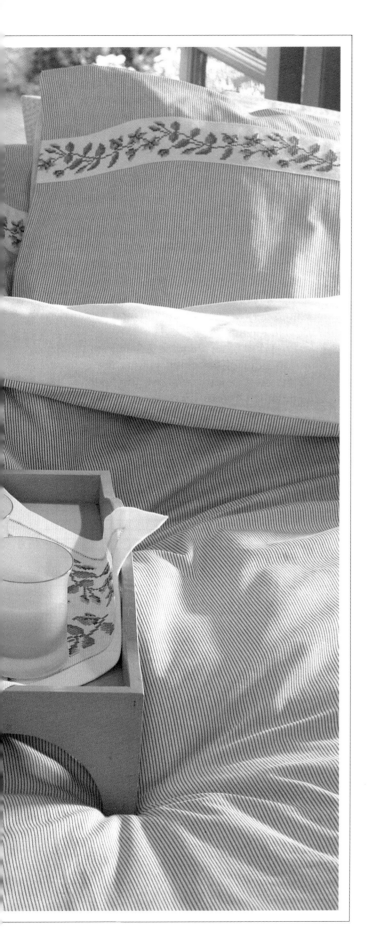

Gentian

TRAYCLOTH
· AND ·
PILLOWCASES

A charming border of gentians
creates a restful and refreshing
design for a set of pillowcases
and a matching traycloth.
The traycloth is neatly finished
with hemstitching, and the
pillow design is embroidered
on a Hardanger strip and then
stitched to purchased
pillowcases – breakfast in bed
could become a habit!

· A VASE OF ·
White Flowers

With its subtle whites, greys
and blues, this would grace
any room or make a
charming wedding gift.

· M A T E R I A L S ·

For the picture, with an embroidered area
measuring approximately 22 × 29cm
(8¾ × 11¾in), set in a frame approximately
48 × 54cm (19¼ × 21½in), you will need:

70 × 75cm (28 × 30in) of beige,
26-count linen
Stranded embroidery cottons, as listed in the
colour key
No 26 tapestry needle
A frame and mount of your choice

NOTE *This design has been worked in Anchor*
yarns; DMC equivalents are also given, but the
end result could be slightly different.

· T H E   E M B R O I D E R Y ·

Prepare and frame the fabric (see page 6),
marking the centre with lines of basting. Cross
stitch from the centre, using two strands of
embroidery cotton in the needle (unless the
key states otherwise), taken over two threads of
the fabric. Finish with the backstitching, using
one strand in the needle.

Carefully steam press the finished embroidery on the wrong side; lace it over a cardboard mount (see page 8), and set it in the
frame and mount of your choice.

A VASE OF WHITE FLOWERS ▶

		DMC	ANCHOR
⊡	White	White	1
⊙	White (one strand)	White	1
⊚	Blue green (one strand)	563	204
⊠	Light blue green	966	206
⊡	Green	913	209
⊟	Light grey green (one strand)	504	213
■	Dark green	561	217
⊅	Silver grey	3072	234
◢	Bright green	702	243
⊡	Light yellowy green	772	259
⧄	Yellowy green	3348	265
⊠	Light blue grey	928	274
⊠	Light blue grey (one strand)	928	274
⧄	Very pale yellow (one strand)	746	275
⊔	Light grey	762	397
⧅	Mid-grey	415	398
◪	Grey	318	399
	Dark grey*	3799	236
⧄	Very light brown	822	830
⊓	Very light brown (one strand)	822	830
⊓	Light brown (one strand)	644	831
⊠	Medium blue grey	927	849
⊠	Medium blue grey (one strand)	927	849
◣	Dark blue grey	926	850
⧄	Dark blue grey (one strand)	926	850
⊠	Light green brown	372	853
⊠	Grey green (one strand)	523	859
	Dark grey green*	502	876
	Dark moss green*	986	246
⊠	Beige	739	885
⊠	Brownish grey	3072	900
⊡	Light yellowy brown (one strand)	738	942
⊔	Yellowy brown (one strand)	437	943

Backstitching: backstitch around the flowers in the large vase with dark grey green, around the flowers in the small vase with bright green, around the leaves and stems of the flowers with dark moss green* and around the vases and bottle with dark grey*; starred colours are used for backstitching only.*

Strawberry
· MAT AND ·
JAM COVER

Delicious home-made
strawberry jam deserves to be
enhanced by a pretty cover and
matching table linen.
The mat, with its circular
design, would make a lovely
table centre, perhaps to set off
an array of cakes and scones, as
well as the jam.
If you choose, you could adapt
the strawberry motif to make
matching napkins.

· M A T E R I A L S ·

For the **tablemat**, measuring 39.5cm (15¾in), you will need:

*45cm (18in) square of yellow 26-count evenweave fabric
Stranded embroidery cottons, as listed in the colour key
No 26 tapestry needle
White sewing cotton*

For the **jam-pot cover**, measuring 26cm (10½in) in diameter, you will need:

*30cm (12in) square of the same fabric as above
Embroidery cotton and needle, as above
90cm (1yd) of red bias binding
50cm (20in) of pink ribbon*

NOTE These designs have been worked in DMC yarns; Anchor equivalents are also given, but the end result could be slightly different.

· T H E   T A B L E M A T ·

Prepare the fabric, marking the centre with basting stitches. Following the chart, embroider the motif, then repeat it three times to complete the circle. Use two strands of embroidery cotton in the needle, and work over two threads of the fabric. Finish with the backstitching, using one or two strands of embroidery cotton, as stated in the key.

Complete the embroidery with the cross stitch outline. Count 24 threads down from point A, and embroider a frame of cross stitches, 36.5cm (14½in) square. Use two strands of rose pink embroidery cotton in the needle, making each stitch over two threads of the fabric, and leaving two threads between each stitch.

Trim the fabric to measure 43.5cm (17½in). Turn a double hem, bringing the foldline five threads out from the cross stitch outline and mitring the corners. Press and baste, and then withdraw three threads from the fabric at each side, to meet at the corners. Darn in the ends at the corners, and then secure the hem with hemstitching (see page 126), stitching over two threads of the fabric.

· J A M - P O T   C O V E R ·

Prepare the fabric, marking the centre with basting stitches, and embroider the motif, centring it on the fabric. Use two strands of embroidery cotton in the needle for the cross stitches, and work over two threads of the fabric. Finish with the backstitching.

Using a plate as a marker, trim the fabric to measure 26cm (10½in) in diameter. Secure the raw edge with the red bias binding. Use the ribbon to tie the cover over the pot.

STRAWBERRY DESIGN		DMC	ANCHOR
⊡	Pale straw	746	275
	Yellow*	726	297
◞	Light pink	957	51
⊵	Pink	892	57
✳	Red	666	46
◹	Very light green	369	206
◺	Bright green	702	226
◉	Green	700	229
⌿	Light green moss	471	266
⊠	Soft green	989	243
	Dark green*	699	923

Backstitching: backstitch around the leaves with dark green and the strawberries with yellow* (both of these colours are used for backstitching only), and stitch around the unripe strawberries with light green.*

Pot Cover

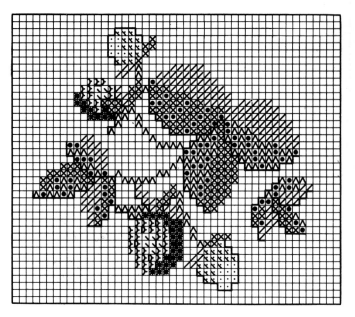

Tablemat

Summer
· BOUQUET ·

A summer's bouquet of garden
and hedgerow flowers
has been captured in time in
this charming embroidery.

· MATERIALS ·

For the picture, with an embroidered area
measuring approximately 25 × 35cm
(10 × 14in), set in a frame approximately
41 × 51cm (16½ × 20½in), you will need:

70 × 80cm (28 × 32in) of white,
26-count linen
Stranded embroidery cottons, as listed in the
colour key
No 26 tapestry needle
A frame and mount of your choice

NOTE This design has been worked in DMC
yarns; Anchor equivalents are also given, but
the end result could be slightly different.

· THE EMBROIDERY ·

Prepare and frame the fabric (see page 6), marking the centre with horizontal and vertical lines of basting. Embroider the cross stitch design, starting from the centre and taking the stitches over two threads of the fabric. For the background, use one strand of embroidery cotton in the needle; for the grey shades in the vase, use two, and for the blue shades in the vase, the flowers, and the butterfly, use three strands. Finish with the backstitching, using one strand of embroidery cotton in the needle.

Carefully steam press the finished embroidery on the wrong side; lace it over a cardboard mount (see page 8), and set it in the frame and mount of your choice.

Top

SUMMER BOUQUET ▶		DMC	ANCHOR
⊡	White	White	1
▣	Very dark pink	309	39
▨	Grey	318	399
◸	Dark pink	335	38
◺	Soft green	368	208
◡	Light grey	415	398
◪	Brown	420	374
⠒	Light yellow	445	289
∨	Light yellowy green	472	253
▯	Light turquoise	519	167
▲	Purple	553	98
⊟	Light purple	554	95
▼	Dark brown	610	375
◎	Dark orange yellow	742	303
△	Orange yellow	743	302
⊟	Pale orange yellow	744	301
◺	Very light grey	762	397
◹	Light pink	776	24
▪	Dark blue	797	133
▽	Blue	798	131
◰	Very light blue	800	128
◳	Light blue	809	129
⊡	Very light pink	818	271
◿	Light yellowy brown	834	874
◣	Orange brown	922	338
◿	Very light green	966	210
◢	Dark green	987	217
◿	Green	988	216
•	Light green	989	261
◺	Pink	3326	25
⊠	Moss green	3347	266
⊞	Light moss green	3348	265

Backstitching: backstitch the green section of the butterfly with light green, and the yellow section with light yellowy brown; along the white petals of the marguerites with dark green; around and in the vase with dark blue; around the light purple flowers with dark pink, and make all remaining backstitches in a matching colour or a shade slightly darker than the surrounding area.

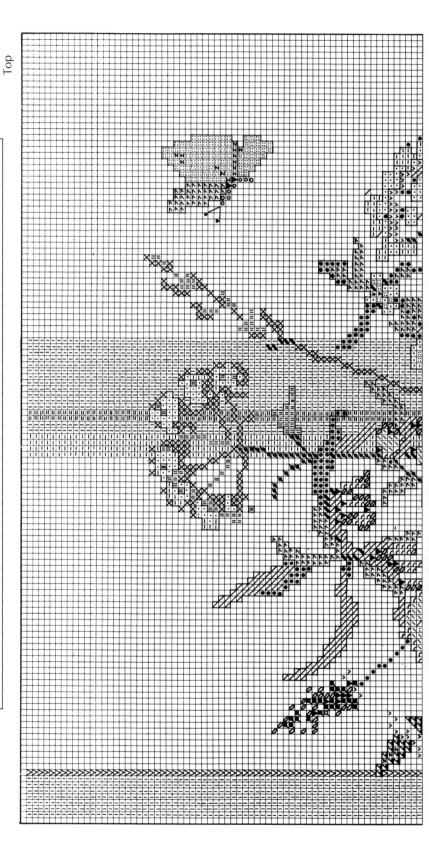

Bottom

A

Trailing Border

· TABLE SET ·

A simple trailing border of tiny flowers and leaves is framed within a double row of cross stitches to make a fresh, pretty tablemat. The napkin echoes the theme with the floral motif in one corner, again emphasized with a simple frame of cross stitches.

· MATERIALS ·

For one **tablemat**, measuring approximately 35 × 44cm (14 × 17½in), you will need:

55 × 65cm (22 × 26in) of 25-count evenweave fabric, in a colour of your choice
Stranded embroidery cottons, as listed in the appropriate colour key
No 26 tapestry needle
White sewing cotton

For one **napkin**, measuring 32cm (12¾in) square, you will need:

40cm (16in) square of white 25-count evenweave fabric
Other materials, as above

NOTE These designs have been worked in DMC yarns; Anchor equivalents are also given, but the end result could be slightly different.

· THE TABLEMAT ·

Starting at A, 9cm (3¾in) in from the raw edge at the bottom and the right-hand side, embroider the trailing border, following the chart (this shows one quarter of the border). Use two strands of cotton in the needle and work over two threads of the fabric. Repeat the chart mirror-wise three times to complete the design.

Next, work a frame of cross stitches four threads out from the outermost stitches of the trailing border. Use two strands of turquoise embroidery cotton in the needle and work over two threads of the fabric, leaving a gap of two threads between each two stitches. Finish the embroidery with a solid line of cross stitches two threads out from the first frame.

Trim the fabric to within 6cm (2¼in) of the outline stitching all around. Turn and baste a double 2cm (¾in) hem all around, mitring the corners, and slipstitch, using the white thread.

· THE NAPKIN ·

Embroider just the corner motif from the chart, working as for the tablemat. Continue the turquoise lines for 23.5cm (9½in) and then turn the corners to complete the square. Work a second, outline square of cross stitches, 10 threads beyond the first. Trim the fabric to within 3cm (1¼in) of the outline stitching and hem as for the tablemat, but making only a double 1cm (⅜in) turning.

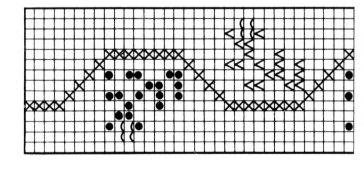

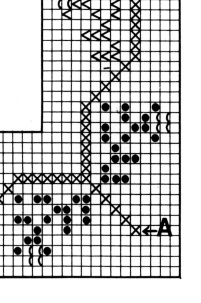

BORDER DESIGN

		DMC	ANCHOR
●	Green	562	210
⊠	Light green	563	207
◖	Pink	776	24
⊠	Turquoise	963	185

Note: for the napkin only, light green is not required.

Two Rose

Two pictures to charm
any rose lover – *Rosa
damascena* 'Celsiana' and
R. 'Lumila'. Either would
be delightful to own, and
both would be a luxury.

· M A T E R I A L S ·
Rosa damascena 'Celsiana' measures
approximately 18.5 × 22.5cm (7½ × 9in) and
R. 'Lumila' measures approximately
17 × 20cm (6¾ × 8in); each is set in a frame
measuring 29.5 × 35.5cm (11¾ × 14¼in),
and for each picture you will need:

*40cm (16in) square of white 25-count
evenweave linen
Stranded embroidery cottons, as listed in the
appropriate colour key
No 26 tapestry needle
A frame of your choice*

*NOTE These designs have been worked in
Anchor yarns; DMC equivalents are also given,
but the end result could be slightly different.*

· T H E E M B R O I D E R Y ·
For each picture, prepare the fabric and stretch
it in a frame, as explained on page 6. Starting
from the centre, embroider the cross stitch
design, using two threads of the stranded
cotton and stitching over two threads of the
fabric. For the backstitching, use one thread of
stranded cotton in the needle throughout.

Carefully steam press the finished embroidery on the wrong side. Lace it over cardboard
(see page 8) and set in your chosen frame.

Rosa Lumila

ROSA 'LUMILA' ▼	DMC	ANCHOR			DMC	ANCHOR
◿ Light brown	3045	373		⊙ Dark pink	223	895
⋈ Brown	3032	832		◢ Very dark pink	221	896
⊢ Very light green	772	842		Dark fuchsia*	309	42
⁖ Beige	3047	852		⫴ Yellowish green	372	945
⌐ Light brownish green	372	853		+ Very light yellowish	3047	956
⊟ Brownish green	371	854		green		
⟍ Light green	524	858		Very dark green*	3362	861
⋁ Grey green	523	859				
⨯ Dark grey green	3363	860				
■ Orange brown	3364	883				
· Light beige	712	885				
⋀ Yellow	676	891				
Ⅰ Light pink	225	893				
⊟ Pink	224	894				

Backstitching: backstitch in and around the roses with dark fuchsia*, and around the hearts of the red roses and all other remaining backstitch lines in very dark green* (both these shades are used for backstitching only).

Backstitching: backstitch in and around the pink roses with dark rose, and in and around the white roses with light grey*; all the remaining backstitches are very dark green* (all of these shades are used for backstitching only).*

Additional Stitches

· FRENCH KNOTS ·

This stitch is shown on some of the diagrams by a small dot. Where there are several French knots, the dots have been omitted to avoid confusion. Where this occurs you should refer to the instructions of the project and the colour photograph.

To work a French knot, bring your needle and cotton out slightly to the right of where you want your knot to be. Wind the thread once or twice around the needle, depending on how big you want your knot to be, and insert the needle to the left of the point where you brought it out.

Be careful not to pull too hard or the knot will disappear through the fabric. The instructions state the number of strands of cotton to be used for the French knots.

· HEMSTITCH ·

This stitch is the traditional way of finishing the hems of embroidered napkins and tablecloths. For a fringed hem, remove a single thread at the hem and stitch along the line as shown. When you have finished, remove the weft threads below the hemstitching, to make the fringe.
Note: When hemstitching Aida and similar fabrics, it is not necessary to remove the initial thread; the stitches can be worked along a line of 'blocks' or groups of threads. As you are stitching blocks instead of single threads, make sure that you refer to the project instructions to discover the number of blocks to work for the hemstitching.

● Bring the needle out on the right side, two threads below the drawn-thread line. Working from left to right, pick up either two or three threads, as shown in the diagram. Bring the needle out again and insert it behind the fabric, to emerge two threads down, ready to make the next stitch. Before reinserting the needle, pull the thread tight, so that the bound threads form a neat group.

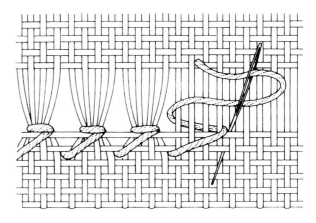

· LADDER VARIATION ·

For the ladder variation of hemstitch, withdraw threads to the required depth, then work hemstitch along each edge, tying groups of threads together in a ladder formation.

· LAZY DAISY ·

Sometimes known as detached chain stitch, this is made in the same way as chain stitch, but with loops either scattered or shaped in a daisy formation. To make each petal, bring the needle out (at the centre of the flower), and reinsert it at the same point, holding the thread down with your thumb to form a loop. Bring the needle up just inside the loop; pull the thread through, and

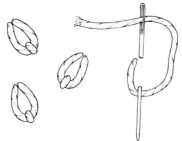

reinsert the needle the other side of the loop, bringing it up again at the centre of the flower, ready for the next petal.

INDEX

SUPPLIERS

For information on your
nearest stockist of embroidery
cotton, contact the following:

DMC

UK
DMC Creative World Limited
62 Pullman Road
Wigston
Leicester LE8 2DY
Telephone: 0533 811040

USA
The DMC Corporation
Port Kearney Bld.
10 South Kearney
N.J. 07032-0650
Telephone: 201 589 0606

AUSTRALIA
DMC Needlecraft Pty
P.O. Box 317
Earlswood 2206
NSW 2204
Telephone: 02599 3088

COATS AND ANCHOR

UK
Kilncraigs Mill
Alloa
Clackmannanshire
Scotland FK10 1EG
Telephone: 0259 723431

USA
Coats & Clark
P.O. Box 27067
Dept CO1
Greenville
SC 29616
Telephone: 803 234 0103

AUSTRALIA
Coats Patons Crafts
Thistle Street
Launceston
Tasmania 7250
Telephone: 00344 4222